PSYCHOLOGY, COUNSELLING AND THERAPEUTIC PRACTICES

PSYCHOLOGY, COUNSELLING AND THERAPEUTIC PRACTICES

Editor

Ramesh Chandra

ISHA BOOKS

DELHI-110 033

Psychology, Counselling and Therapeutic Practices

Rs. 850

ISBN: 81-8205-143-6

Published in 2004 in India by
Isha Books, D-43, Prithviraj Road,
Adarsh Nagar, Delhi-110 033

Laser Typesetting at : Shree Vaishnavi Creations, Delhi
Printed at : Chawla Offset Press, Delhi

Contents

Preface

Both psychotherapy and counselling are psychological processes that use the same theoretical models. Each stresses the need to value the client as a person, to listen carefully and sympathetically to what they have to say, and to foster the capacity for self-help and personal responsibility. To date psychotherapy and counselling have their origins more in dealing with the problems of the sub-normal and normal that in trying to assist well-functioning people to develop their full human potential.

Psychotherapeutic and counselling techniques aims to cure severe mental disorders. They are also having remedial, developmental and growth goals. Remedial goals focus on helping clients overcome deficiencies to normal functioning. Such clients, who form a minority of the population, may be anywhere from severely to moderately disturbed in their ability to function effectively. Developmental goals focus on the needs of ordinary people rather than those of the more disturbed minority. Such goals may focus on preventing negative outcomes and on promoting positive changes associated with developmental tasks at various stages over the life-span: for instance, making friends at school, leaving home, finding a partner, establishing a career, raising children and adjusting to old age. Growth goals focus on helping clients attain higher levels of functioning than the average.

The principles and practises of counselling and psychotherapeutic techniques are elaborately discussed in the present book. It will serve as a highly informative reference tool for psychologists, counsellors, teachers and students.

Editor

1

Psychotherapy and Counselling

Therapy is derived from the Greek word 'therapeia' meaning healing. Attempts to differentiate between counselling and psychotherapy are never.wholly successful. Because counselling and therapy represent diverse rather than uniform knowledge and activities, it is more accurate to think of coun-selling approaches and psychological therapies. Attempts to distinguish counselling from therapy include observations that therapy deals more with mental disorders than counselling, that therapy is longer-term and deeper, and that therapy is predominantly associated with medical settings. However, matters are not this clear-cut.

Many counsellors work in medical settings, have clients with recognized mental disorders and do longer-term work that is sometimes of a psychodynamic nature. Syme rightly suggests that there is huge overlap between coun-selling and therapy. As an illustration of perceived overlap, the Psychotherapy and Counselling Federation of Australia promulgates 'A definition of coun-selling and psychotherapy' as a single statement.

Both counselling and therapy are psychological processes that use the same theoretical models. Each stresses the need to value the client as a person, to listen carefully and sympatheti-cally to what they have to say, and to foster the capacity for self-help and personal responsibility.

Goals

Let's consider some different ways of looking at goals for counselling and therapy. Leaving aside severe mental disorders, a common breakdown of goals is that between remedial, developmental and growth. Remedial goals focus on helping clients overcome deficiencies to normal functioning. Such clients, who form a minority of the population, may be anywhere from severely to moderately disturbed in their ability to function effectively.

Developmental goals focus on the needs of ordinary people rather than those of the more disturbed minority. Such goals may focus on preventing negative outcomes and on promoting positive changes associated with developmental tasks at various stages over the life-span: for instance, making friends at school, leaving home, finding a partner, establishing a career, raising children and adjusting to old age.

Growth goals focus on helping clients attain higher levels of functioning than the average. In relation to this remedial, developmental and growth distinction, it is possible to look at human functioning in three broad categories - sub-normal, normal and supra-normal - with, at any given moment, individuals being placed somewhere along this continuum. Sub-normal functioning is that where individuals are psychologically distressed and have problems that are more severe than the normal run of the population.

Some such clients might suffer from the mental disorders that are listed in the American Psychiatric Association's Diagnostic and Statistical Manual of Mental Disorders. Normal functioning is that where people are capable of conventional adaptation to the societies in which they live. Such individuals may still experience problems for which counselling and therapy is appropriate: for instance, relationship problems, stress problems and study problems.

Some clients who are functioning well may want to function even better. Supra-normal functioning refers to going above, beyond or transcending normal human functioning. Drawing on Eastern and Western traditions, qualities of supra-normal functioning include equanimity, autonomy, mental purification, human sympathy, honesty both with oneself and others, inner strength, heightened concentration and compassionate or selfless service.

To date therapy and counselling have their origins more in dealing with the problems of the sub-normal and normal that in trying to assist well-functioning people to develop their full human potential. All the major counselling and therapy approaches have been developed by psychiatrists and clinical psychologists. There has yet to be a major therapeutic approach developed by professionals, such as counselling psychologists or counsellors, who predominantly deal with normal client populations, let alone superior functioning ones.

Another way of looking at goals for counselling and therapy is to consider them in terms of objectives for different clients. There are five levels of goals for those using counselling skills. The first or supportive listening goal is to provide clients with a sense of being understood and affirmed. Attaining this goal requires counsellors and therapists to be skilled at listening to clients, taking their perspectives, and sensitively showing them that they have been heard accurately.

Counsellors with good listening skills can comfort, ease suffering, heal psychological wounds and act as sounding boards for moving forward. Furthermore, counsellors should be careful never to underestimate the power of effective listen-ing both for comforting and for empowering clients. Second, there is the managing a problem situation goal. Clients may want help dealing with specific situations that are problematic for them. In addition, counselling may best proceed if a specific situation within a larger problem is addressed rather than trying to deal with the whole problem. With a shy college student client, rather than focus on the broader problem of shyness, counsellor and client might concentrate on a particular shyness situation of importance to the client, such as either asking or being asked by a particular person for a date.

Third, there is the problem management goal. Though some problems are limited, many other problems can be larger and more complex than specific situations within them. Take the example of a client with children going through a divorce. Here dimensions of the problem might include obtaining a just divorce settlement, maintaining self-esteem, relationships with children, a possible move of home, and learning to live as a single adult again.

Fourth, there is the altering poor skills that sustain problems goal. Other terms for poor skills include problematic, deficient or insufficiently effective skills. Here the assumption is that problems tend to repeat themselves.

In the past clients may have been repeating underlying mind skills and communication or action skills deficiencies and are at risk of continuing to do so again. For instance, workers who keep moving jobs may again and again set themselves up to become unhappy or to get fired.

Following are the six central mind skills

1 *Creating rules* People's unrealistic rules make irrational demands on them, others, and the environment: for instance, 'I must always be happy', 'Others must look after me', and 'My environment should not contain any suffering'. Instead they can develop realistic rules: for instance, 'I prefer to be happy much of the time, but it is unrealistic to expect this all the time.'

2 *Creating perceptions* People can avoid perceiving themselves and others either too negatively or too positively. They can create compassionate rather than competitive or negative perceptions of the human race. They can distinguish between fact and inference and make their inferences as accurate as possible.

3 *Creating self-talk* Instead of talking to themselves negatively before, during and after specific situations, people can acknowledge that they have choices and make coping self-statements that assist them to stay calm and cool, establish their goals, coach them in what to do, and affirm their strengths, skills and support factors.

4 *Creating visual images* People can use visual images to calm themselves down, assist them in acting competently to attain their goals, and help them to resist giving in to bad habits.

5 *Creating explanations* People can explain the causes of events accurately. They avoid assuming too much

responsibility by internalizing, 'It's all my fault', or externalizing, 'It's all other people's fault'.

6 *Creating expectations* People are realistic about the risks and rewards of future actions.They assess threats and dangers accurately. They avoid distorting relevant evidence with unwarranted optimism or pessimism. Their expectations about how well they will communicate and act are accurate.

Thus the problem is not just the pre-senting problem, but the poor skills that create, sustain or worsen the problem. The therapeutic goal is to equip the client with skills not just to manage a present problem, but to prevent and deal with future similar ones.

Fifth, there is the bringing about a changed philosophy of life goal. Here, clients can use their skills not only to prevent and manage the problems that brought them to counselling, but to deal with a range of other problems and situations that they may face in future. Their new and improved skills have become integrated into how they think about and approach their daily lives. The difference in how they think, feel and communicate can be so fundamental that it can be equated to a change in their philosophy of life.

Though many of these skills are also relevant to working with clients at both ends of the spectrum - those with mental dis-orders and those seeking to attain supra-normal levels of functioning.

However, as all physical illnesses (e.g. cancer, heart disease, asthma) may have psychological aspects or complications. There was a high degree of consensus on four physical conditions for which they would welcome guidance.

— chronic pain,

— chronic fatigue,

— gastrointestinal disorders (e.g. irritable bowel syndrome)

— gynaecological presentations (e.g. pre-menstrual syndrome, pelvic pain, menopausal vasomotor symptoms)

These guideline therefore does not address the use of psychological therapies in the following situations:

— disorders in childhood and adolescence,

— psychoses including schizophrenia,

— mania and bipolar disorder,

— alcohol and other drug addictions,

— sexual dysfunction & paraphilias

— organic brain syndromes and acquired brain injury

— learning disability

Decisions about these exclusions were made on pragmatic grounds, to focus on common mental health problems in adults. Exclusion from the guideline does not imply that psychological therapies are unhelpful or inappropriate in these conditions, simply that they are beyond the scope of this particular guideline. For example, psychological therapies have been developed specifically to help people with schizophrenia or alcohol problems.

The guideline only considers the choice of psychological therapy and does not consider pharmacological treatments. In general, prescribed medication is not a contra-indication for psychological therapy (or vice versa), and separate consideration will need to be given to pharmacological treatments.

Cost effectiveness of psychological therapies is clearly an important element of treatment choice decisions. However, true economic appraisal in this field is extremely sparse and basic methodological issues are only now being addressed by researchers and health economists.

There are many types of psychological treatment and the range of 'brand name' therapies can be confusing for the non-specialist. Psychological therapies are provided by members of different professional disciplines, including clinical psychologists and psychiatrists, specially trained mental health nurses, occupational therapists, art and drama therapists, counsellors and psychotherapists. Some therapists have generic roles, providing therapy as an integral part of care programmes within mental health teams. Others provide stand-alone services. There is a wide range of training routes to competence as a psychological therapist.

Within this broad family of therapies, there are two main traditions, psychotherapy and counselling. The distinction between the two is blurred, as they lie on a continuum, such that for each type of psychological therapy there is a corresponding form of counselling (psychodynamic psychotherapy - psychodynamic counselling, cognitive behaviour therapy - cognitive behavioural counselling, etc.). In essence, different forms of psychotherapy have evolved to offer remediation of mental health problems and symptoms by structured interventions.

Types of Psychotherapies

Different forms of counselling emphasise the individual's resources rather than psychopathology, with a focus on a reflective, experiential process. Here the patient's concerns are rephrased and clarified in order that he or she may develop a greater sense of well being and cope with life difficulties differently. There is emphasis on mental health promotion rather than 'treating disorders'. The terminological confusion is exacerbated by the common practice of denoting all psychological therapy delivered in primary care as 'counselling'. In fact, a number of 'counsellors' employed in primary care are qualified psychotherapists.

Cognitive Behaviour Therapy (CBT)

This refers to the pragmatic combination of concepts and techniques from cognitive and behaviour therapies, common in clinical practice. Behaviour therapy is a structured therapy originally derived from learning theory, which seeks to solve problems and relieve symptoms by changing behaviour and the environmental factors which control behaviour. Graded exposure to feared situations is one of the commonest behavioural treatment methods and is used in a range of anxiety disorders.

Cognitive therapy is a structured treatment approach derived from cognitive theories. Cognitive techniques (such as challenging negative automatic thoughts) and behavioural techniques (such as activity scheduling and behavioural experiments) are used with the main aim of relieving symptoms by changing maladaptive thoughts and beliefs.

Psychoanalytic Therapies

A number of different therapies draw on psychoanalytic theories, although they differ in terms of technique. Focal psychodynamic therapy identifies a central conflict arising from early experience that is being re-enacted in adult life producing mental health problems. It aims to resolve this through the vehicle of the relationship with the therapist giving new opportunities for emotional assimilation and insight. This form of therapy is often time-limited, with anxiety aroused by the ending of therapy being used to illustrate how re-awakened feelings about earlier losses, separations and disappointments may be experienced differently.

Psychoanalytic psychotherapy is a longer-term process (usually a year or more) of allowing unconscious conflicts opportunity to be re-enacted in the relationship with the therapist and, through interpretation, worked through in a developmental process.

Systemic Therapy

Systemic and family therapists understand individual problems by considering the relevance of family relationships and the impact of the wider social and economic context on people's lives, their wellbeing and their mental health. Therapeutic work is undertaken with individuals, couples, or families and may include consultation to wider networks such as other professionals working with the individual or the family.

Therapy aims to identify and explore patterns of belief and behaviour in roles and relationships and therapists actively intervene to enable people to decide where change would be desirable and to facilitate the process of establishing new, more fulfilling and useful patterns. Therapists may work in teams using live consultation or as sole practitioners using retrospective consultation. Therapy is often relatively short term.

Eclectic Therapies

The resulting therapy is pragmatic, tailored to the individual. These generic therapies often emphasise important non-specific factors (such as building the therapeutic alliance and engendering hope). By their nature, they are more idiosyncratic and difficult to standardise for the purposes of randomised controlled trials research.

Integrative Therapy

An integrative therapy differs from eclectic approaches, as it is a formal theoretical and methodological integration of, for example, behavioural, cognitive, humanistic or psychodynamic approaches. These therapies are therefore amenable to research. One such approach is cognitive analytic therapy.

Other types of therapy practised include existential, humanistic, process-experiential (client-centred), feminist, personal construct, art therapy, drama therapy, transactional analysis and group analysis.

Counselling

Counselling is a systematic process which gives individuals an opportunity to explore, discover and clarify ways of living more resourcefully, with a greater sense of well being. Counselling may be concerned with addressing and resolving specific problems, making decisions, coping with crises, working through conflict, or improving relationships with others. Counsellors may practice within any of the therapeutic approaches listed above, using psychodynamic counselling, cognitive behavioural counselling, systemic counselling and so on.

However, most are influenced by humanistic, process-experiential and psychodynamic principles. The work of most counsellors is generalist (analogous to general practice) and is not necessarily linked to diagnostic categories. Many counsellors work in primary care, but they are increasingly found in secondary care settings. A broad distinction can be made between generic and specific counselling. The latter may be specific to a therapeutic model (for example, psychodynamic counselling) or a life crisis (for example, bereavement counselling).

In relation to specific life crisis issues, there are many voluntary sector counselling agencies (Relate, bereavement agencies, sexual abuse survivor groups etc) to whom GPs commonly refer patients with mental health problems.

Evidence of the effectiveness of psychotherapy and counselling for people with particular diagnoses, including the differential effectiveness of specific types of therapy. The diagnostic areas/presenting problems considered were:

— depression including postnatal depression;

— anxiety disorders including generalised anxiety, panic and agoraphobia, social phobia, post-traumatic stress disorder, and obsessive compulsive disorder;

- — eating disorders;
- — personality disorders;
- — Somatic presentations including chronic pain, chronic fatigue, gastrointestinal problems and gynaecological problems.

Evidence about the impact of other factors on therapy outcome. Other factors include: comorbidity, chronicity, severity and features of the presenting problem; demographics, family situation, psychological characteristics, therapeutic alliance, attitude to therapy and treatment history of the client; length, setting and process of the therapy.

Psychological treatment has been found effective in the treatment of depression in general adult and older adult populations, including in inpatient care. Cognitive behaviour therapy and interpersonal therapy in particular have been found efficacious in the treatment of depression, with best evidence for cognitive behaviour therapy.

Behavioural therapy, problem-solving therapy, group therapy and marital and family interventions have all shown some evidence of efficacy. Psychodynamic-interpersonal therapy has also shown evidence of effectiveness. Time-limited depression-targeted psychotherapies are efficacious when transferred from psychiatric to primary care settings. Exposure-based treatment and CBT have shown efficacy in the treatment of agoraphobia, although exposure may be less effective on measures of panic.

Social phobia

Exposure and cognitive therapy are effective for the treatment of social phobia.

Generalised anxiety disorder

Cognitive and behavioural therapies are effective in treating GAD.

Obsessive Compulsive Disorder

Behaviour therapy (or exposure with response prevention) and cognitive therapy appear to be efficacious in the treatment of OCD, although there is disagreement over which is more effective according to the available evidence. These psychological treatments appear to produce results similar to those achieved by drug treatments. Behavioural treatment may be less effective in treating depressive symptoms than anxiety symptoms in OCD.

Eating disorders

For the treatment of bulimia, evidence suggests that psychological therapy is efficacious. The efficacy of cognitive/cognitive-behavioural therapy has been established; less research has been carried out on other forms of therapy, but there are indications that family therapy and interpersonal approaches may be effective. Focus on relationships in therapy has been associated with good outcome.

Cognitive behaviour therapy and Rational Emotive Therapy were found effective for pre-menstrual syndrome. Pelvic pain benefited from a cognitive behavioural approach. Vasomotor symptoms in menopause were reduced by applied relaxation therapy.

Personality Disorders

There is little comparative outcome research on the treatment of personality disorders with psychotherapy, and no high quality reviews were identified. There are promising developments in psychotherapeutic treatment in this field, but most results are from cohort studies. A Cochrane review found some evidence of efficacy in reducing self-harm for problem-solving therapy, for the provision of an emergency card, and from a single study of dialectical behaviour therapy. A trial of psychoanalytically informed partial hospitalisation compared with standard psychiatric care showed reduction in self harm and suicide attempts in patients with personality disorder after 6 months treatment, maintained until the end of treatment at 18 months.

Co-morbidity

The therapy for mental health problems may have poorer outcomes when they co-exist with personality disorders. However, avoidant and dependent personality disorders were positive indicators for supportive therapy.

Chronicity

No consistent effect of chronicity of disorder has been established.

Features of disorders

There is little evidence on the effects of features or subtypes of particular disorders. Generalised type social phobia, and restrictive type bulimia have been associated with poorer outcome. Most research does not indicate an association between endogenous type depression and poorer outcome.

Generally, no effect of gender or age on outcome has been found. Quality of current family environment may be predictive of therapy outcome, with poorer family environment reducing effectiveness of group/individual treatments, but enhancing effectiveness of couple-based treatments.

Patients are treated in primary care if they have mild, stress-related problems or adjustment to life events, or problems with physical health or health behaviours, requiring supportive therapy. Other good reasons for not referring out of primary care include patient choice, a previously good response to primary care treatment or intolerance of psychological treatment. The level of skills, support and supervision available in the primary care setting would also be determining factors.

Many patients can be treated in primary care settings if an appropriate therapy is available and if this is acceptable to the patient. Patient preference or demand for a secondary service should also be taken into account. Appropriate referral to a community mental health team (CMHT). In addition to the general criteria for referral to a secondary service, criteria include: known to the CMHT, have had a relapse of a chronic mental health problem, need multi-agency work, are suicidal, self-harming, or pose a risk to others, particularly patients with psychosis, or who are mentally disordered offenders.

In addition to the general criteria for referral to a secondary service, criteria include: have obsessive compulsive disorders, personality disorders or repeated consultations for health anxiety, where patient shows some motivation for a psychological therapy, and desire for change. Although these principles were reached by structured expert consensus, the research evidence base describes therapies in a mixture of settings, and there is little specific evidence on the impact of location.

Psychological therapy should be routinely considered as a treatment option when assessing mental health problems. This principle is important in decisions by GPs and their patients about the option of psychological therapy, because 'therapeutic alliance' is the single best predictor of benefit. A good working relationship in therapy does not necessarily mean the absence of conflict or difficulty, but a fundamental agreement on the goals and tasks of therapy and some level of commitment to the relationship. If this is lacking, the therapy is less likely to be helpful, whatever other research evidence may recommend it in general terms. If this occurs, a second opportunity to establish a working relationship is advisable.

The issue of optimal treatment length is complex, but referrers and patients often ask for guidance on what to expect. Some service commissioners have only been prepared to fund very brief therapies (e.g. six sessions), although there is no research evidence to suggest that this is an adequate trial of therapy for most moderate to severe problems. Exceptions may be uncomplicated phobias and panic disorder without agoraphobia.

There is a risk of unwarranted and stereotypical assumptions being made about which types of people are most likely to benefit from psychological therapy, e.g. middle-class or well-educated people, or women, or people under 50. There is generally no consistent research evidence for these assumptions.

Many physical illnesses have a psychological component, and patients may respond to individual therapy if they are willing to participate. There are four conditions: chronic pain, chronic fatigue, gastro-intestinal disorders and gynaecological disorders. The best evidence so far, in a quickly developing field, is for cognitive behaviour therapy in the treatment of chronic pain and chronic fatigue. For irritable bowel syndrome, promising results have been obtained with psychodynamic-interpersonal therapy, cognitive behaviour therapy, psychodynamic psychotherapy and hypnosis.

Generic counselling is not recommended as the main intervention for severe and complex mental health problems or personality disorders. Routine debriefing shortly after a traumatic event is unlikely to help prevent post traumatic stress disorder and is not recommended. Psychological intervention should be considered for other somatic complaints with a psychological component, such as irritable bowel syndrome and gynaecological complaints (pre-menstrual syndrome, pelvic pain).

Self-regulatory Model for Psychotherapy and Counselling

Counselling and psychotherapy professionals work within a clearly contracted, principled relationship to enable their clients to explore and resolve a wide range of personal and relational issues. Good therapists facilitate the development of clients' life skills, self-management and their capacity for healthy relationships. Undergo in-depth training to develop their understanding, knowledge and experience of human behaviour, therapeutic capacities and ethical and professional boundaries

Work with individuals, couples, families and groups in the public and private sectors. Use advanced interpersonal skills to work with current problems, immediate crises or long-term difficulties. Respect their clients and their clients' values, beliefs, uniqueness and right to selfdetermination

Counsellors and psychotherapists are unique within the mental health field with respect to undertaking in-depth training, usually at a post-graduate level, in counselling and psychotherapeutic theory and skills, as well as their mandatory requirements for ongoing clinical supervision for the duration of the therapist's career. While counselling and psychotherapy overlap considerably, there are some distinctive differences.

The focus of counselling is more likely to be on specific problems or changes in life adjustment. Psychotherapists are more likely to work intensively with deeper issues and/or more deeply disturbed clients who are seen more frequently and over a longer period of time. Clinical supervision is undertaken by a practitioner through regular sessions with a senior colleague, either individually or as part of a small group.

Professional supervision is an important quality assurance measure to enhance client outcomes and ensure competent and ethical practice, as well as providing a supportive and educative role for the supervisee. It is recognised that a wide range of professions may use a variety of counselling skills as part of their practice, and that the term counselling is part of everyday language with different meaning in different contexts. This has led to difficulties in reaching consensus about the distinctive nature of counselling and psychotherapy as a profession.

Compared with most other health professions, counselling and psychotherapy are in a relatively early stage of development as a profession, providing us with both opportunities and challenges in self-definition.

There have been a number of initiatives to develop the counselling psychotherapy professions in Australia through formation of meta-structures and through establishing bodies for credentialing or 'recognising' fully trained professionals, one of which is the Australian Board of Certified Counsellors (ABCC). There have been a wide variety of initiatives to bring together some theoretically aligned groups within the psychotherapy field.

Some examples include the establishment of Gestalt Australia New Zealand (GANZ), which represented a joining together of all the major gestalt therapy training bodies to form one national professional association for gestalt therapists. A number of psychoanalytic and psychodynamic groups undertook similar tasks and we have seen a consolidation of associations in this area, although there are still a variety of bodies.

Psychotherapy and Counselling Federation of Australia (PACFA) initiative was unique in setting out from the very start to promote principles of collaboration, consultation, dialogue, and inclusiveness and to allow the structure of the organisation to emerge from open and consensual decision-making processes among long-standing but diverse professional associations. It is the only professional body in Australia that can legitimately claim to have developed out of wide consensus within the broad field and to work collaboratively for the interests of the whole field of psychotherapy and counselling professionals.

There are no competing national peak bodies representing the combined psychotherapy and counselling professions. Other national bodies have developed from narrower sections of the professional community to serve a particular sector and have chosen to remain outside the PACFA umbrella. To date, these bodies have been made up of counselling associations. No major psychotherapy specific bodies have been identified that are not already a Member Association of PACFA.

The non-PACFA counselling bodies that have developed include the Australian Association of Career Counsellors, the Australian Board of Certified Counsellors, the Australian Counselling Association, and the Australian Society of Rehabilitation Counsellors. These groups will be formally consulted about these issues of developing a more comprehensive model of selfregulation of the profession. PACFA was established in 1998 with the following primary goals:

— To unite the field of counselling and psychotherapy through collaboration and consensus processes, as well as respecting the valuable diversity of specialisations within the field;

— To act as a peak body, allowing a united voice and greater lobbying power to advance the profession and form effective professional partnerships;

— To establish and regularly review standards for training, supervision, ongoing profession development and ethical practice;

— To develop an accessible Register of practitioners that informs consumers and professionals, provides professional accountability, and has mechanisms in place to foster protection of the public;

— To be open to review of processes and function to optimise achievement of its core functions, and meet the changing needs of government, the health system, other professional bodies and consumers.

The regulation of health professions has emerged historically as a process of exerting various forms of control or influence over the provision of health services. Regulation has been proposed to address various aspects of profession practice, including ethical standards and quality of services or products, as well as market entry, competitive practices, market structures, and remuneration. Baldwin and Cave identified five principles that should govern regulatory systems. They should:

1. Have a clear and legitimate purpose;
2. Have an appropriate scheme of accountability, both to the public in general and to those who are regulated;
3. Be fair, consistent, accessible and open;
4. Operate with sufficient expertise;
5. Be efficient

Accountability needs to be provided to government, the public and those who are regulated, along with an appropriate appeals mechanism. Targeting refers to the appropriate application of rules to the specific context, avoidance of universal approaches, flexibility of enforcement, and modification or elimination of regulations that are ineffective or outdated. Consistency involves compatibility of written rules with activities of other regulators and existing regulations, consistency with trade practices and legal precedents, and consistency of enforcement by appropriate authorities.

The principle of proportionality requires that penalties for breaking the rules should be appropriate, and the impact of regulation should achieve a balance between risk and cost. Different forms of regulation have emerged in response to different historical contexts as well as different requirements and characteristics of particular professions. Many of the longer established health professions (e.g. nursing, medicine, physiotherapy, dentistry, psychology) are governed in all states of Australia by statutory legislation, which generally gives title protection and in some cases protection of practice techniques.

The perceived advantages of statutory regulation are that it provides increased recognition of the profession, has the potential to restrict who can use the professional title (e.g. counsellor or psychotherapist), and therefore provides the public with greater assurance that practicing professionals do meet accepted standards of training and practice. Disadvantages of statutory regulation include the loss of autonomy for the profession, with the rules and structures being imposed from outside the profession, and higher administrative and monitoring costs.

Statutory regulation can involve varying levels of self-regulation nested within the legal framework. The incorporation of self-regulatory components within a regulatory framework is seen to be useful in building compliance and improving implementation of enforcement of the regulatory processes. Self-regulatory models are valued as providing for greater professional autonomy, flexibility, and providing for governance by those with appropriate expertise. The relevant professionals are able to use their 'insider knowledge' to decide on and enforce standards, are able to respond more quickly to changing circumstances (without waiting for changes in legislation), and involve lower costs.

One of the biggest challenges to a self-regulatory model is the voluntary nature of participation in and compliance with the system - how to persuade professionals to voluntarily comply, when there may be few incentives to support this and increased cost to the professional.

Self-regulation generally involves the formation of a professional incorporated body or association with voluntary membership, supported by voluntary standards and codes of practice, and a recognised and accredited body of knowledge. The effectiveness of self-regulation relies on voluntary compliance by members of the group and works best when there are sufficient 'sanctions within the industry to require compliance'. However, since membership of such professional associations is voluntary, there may be no effect upon a practitioner's business if they are expelled from such an association for professional misconduct.

Some counsellors and psychotherapists are registered as psychiatrists, psychologists, doctors, nurses, etc., and are therefore already subject to statutory regulation. The majority of counselling and psychotherapy practitioners, however, are not subject to statutory registration requirements in any state or territory and there are no barriers to entry to the profession. Law does not restrict use of the titles 'counsellor' and 'psychotherapist', and practitioners using these titles have varied levels and types of training and expertise.

One of the main purposes of self-regulation is to provide greater protection for the public through the profession achieving consensus about and monitoring standards of training and practice. To achieve this end, it is highly desirable that the self-regulation process does in fact encompass the whole field, rather than having factions with considerable differences in structure, process and terminology, each making competing claims. Such a situation makes it much more difficult for the public to be able to make informed choices.

Since its inception in 1998, PACFA has established a cohesive peak body representing a substantial majority of professional associations for psychotherapists and counsellors. PACFA has promoted well-developed consensus standards for training and practice, and has been consistently encouraged by a broad range of government bodies

That self-regulation is the most appropriate model of regulation for the professions of psychotherapy and counselling at this time in Australia. That PACFA explore the feasibility of establishing an independent self-regulatory structure for a wider group of allied and/or complementary health professions. State-based statutory registration boards regulate health professions such as psychology, nursing and medicine. The principles that underlie such boards are:

— *Accountability*: registration boards should be accountable to the community for their decisions and operations.

— *Transparency*: the decision-making processes of registration boards should be open, clear, and understandable to both consumers and professionals Fairness: registration boards should maintain an acceptable balance between protection of patients/ consumer rights and interests, and those of the regulated health professionals

— *Effectiveness*: the regulatory system should be effective in protecting the public from harm and supporting and fostering the provision of high quality care Efficiency: the resources expended and the administrative burden imposed by the health professions regulatory system should be justified in terms of the benefits to the Victorian community

— *Flexibility*: the regulatory system should be able to respond to emerging issues in a timely manner as the health care system evolves and the roles and functions of health professionals change Consistency: there should be consistency across Australian states and territories in the regulatory arrangements for the health professions. It is desirable that non-statutory regulated health professions such as psychotherapy and counselling develop a set of self-regulatory mechanisms that incorporate these principles as much as possible.

The most common form of self-regulation involves individual professional bodies developing their own structures for regulating the profession. This would involve developing their own training, qualification and practice criteria for registration, and their own complaints handling mechanisms.

2

Essentials of Counselling Skills

One meaning of the word 'skills' pertains to areas of skill: for instance, lis-tening skills or disclosing skills. Another meaning refers to level of competence, for instance, skilled or unskilled in an area of skill. However, competence in a skill is best viewed not as an either/or matter in which counsellors either possess or do not possess a skill. Rather, within a skills area it is preferable to think of counsellors as possessing good skills or poor skills or a mixture of the two.

In all skills areas counsellors are likely to possess mixtures of strengths and deficiencies. For instance, in the skills area of listening, counsellors may be good at understanding clients but poor at showing their understanding. Similarly, in just about all areas of their functioning, clients will possess a mixture of poor and good skills. A third meaning of skill relates to the knowledge and sequence of choices entailed in implementing the skill. The essential element of any skill is the ability to make and implement sequences of choices to achieve objectives.

For instance, if counsellors are to be good at listening deeply and accurately to clients, they have to make and implement effective choices in this skills area. The object of counselling and therapy skills training, practical placement work and supervision is to help students in the skills areas targeted by their training programmes to move more in the direction of making good rather than poor choices. For example, in the skills area of active listening the objective would be to enable students to make good choices in the process not only of understanding clients but also in showing that under-standing to them.

When thinking of any area of counsellor or client communication, there are two main considerations: first, what are the components of skilled external behaviour; and second, what interferes with or enhances enacting that behav-iour? Thus a counselling and therapy skill like active listening consists both of skilled interpersonal communication and skilled intrapersonal mental processing.

The term 'cognitive behaviour' can obscure the point that outer behaviour originates in the mind and that, as a consequence, both thinking and behaviour are fundamentally mental processes. Counselling skills involve mental processing both to guide external behaviour and to ensure thinking that supports rather than undermines skilled external communication. Let's take the skill of active listening. To some extent it is easy to describe the central elements of the external com-munication involved.

Thus counselling and therapy skills are both mind and communication skills. In reality, some of the mind skills overlap. For instance, all of the skills, even visualizing, involve self-talk. However, here self-talk refers to self-statements relevant to coping with specific situations. Interrelationships between skills can also be viewed on the dimension of depth. Communication and action skills involve observable behaviours. They are what people do and how they do it rather than what and how they feel and think. For instance, it is one thing for counsellors to feel human sympathy for clients, and another to act on this feeling.

Communication and action skills vary by area of application: for instance, listening skills, summarizing skills, challenging skills and coaching skills.There are five main ways in which counsellors and clients can send communication and action skills messages:

1 *Verbal messages:* Messages that people send with words.

2 *Vocal messages:* Messages that people send through their voices: for example, through volume, articulation, pitch, emphasis and speech rate.

3 *Bodily messages:* Messages that people send with their bodies: for instance, through gaze, eye contact, facial expression, posture, gestures, physical proximity and clothes and grooming.

4 *Touch messages:* A special category of body messages. Messages that people send with touch through the parts of body that they use, what parts of another's body they touch, how gentle or firm they are, and whether or not they have permission.

5 *Action-taking messages:* Messages that people send when they are not face-to-face with clients, for example sending letters, e-mails or invoices.

Essential Skills

Essence means the indispensable quality or element identifying a thing or defining its character. One way to answer the question of what are essential counselling and therapy skills is to look for common factors that characterize successful counselling. Some common factors may concern clients: for example, do they genuinely want change and are they prepared to work hard to attain it? Other factors reside in the counsellors, for example do they pos-sess the capacity to be authentic and present in their relationships with clients, to demonstrate empathy and warmth, and to encourage positive expectations in them? Still other factors may form part of the therapeutic process.

For example, clients will benefit from counsellors having the skills to provide them with the opportunity to share and reflect on problems, to express and explore their feelings in an accepting emotional climate, to gain new perspectives and insights, to assume more personal responsibility for their lives and choices, and to discover ways of improving their thinking, communicating and acting. Some essential counselling and therapy skills vary according to clients' dif-fering levels of vulnerability: for example, clients badly wounded by past emotional deprivations require more nurturing and healing than those either less badly treated or more emotionally resilient.

Still other essential skills vary according to the nature of clients' problems: for example, phobic clients require a different kind of counselling to depressed clients. Another way of looking at essential counselling skills is to focus on the skills appropriate for each stage of the counselling process. Essential counselling and therapy skills are communication skills, accompanied by appropriate mental processes, offered by counsellors and therapists in order to develop collaborative working relationships with clients, identify problems, clarify and expand understanding of these problems, and, where appropriate, to assist clients to develop and imple-ment strategies for changing how they think, communicate/act and feel so that they can attain more of their human potential.

The British Association for Counselling and Psychotherapy's accredited counsellor training courses are required to provide students with a core theore-tical model as well as opportunities for comparison with other counselling approaches. Theoretical models provide one way of answering questions concerning the reasons why coun-sellors select and use particular skills.

Theoretical models of counselling approaches may be viewed as possess-ing four main dimensions if they are to be effectively described:

(1) a statement of the basic concepts or assumptions underlying the theory;

(2) an explanation of the acquisition of helpful and unhelpful behaviour;

(3) an explanation of the maintenance of helpful and unhelpful behaviour; and

(4) an explanation of how to help clients change their behaviour and consolidate their gains when therapy ends.

Elements of the change and consolidation dimension include coun-selling goals, process, relationship, interventions, case material and further developments. The basic concepts, acquisition and maintenance dimensions constitute a counselling approach's model of human development and the change and consolidation dimension its model of counselling practice. The model of human development should be internally consistent with and provide the underlying rationale for explaining the model of practice.

Many issues surround the relevance of theory to practice. One such issue is the degree to which the different theoretical positions possess common factors in their models of human development that are obscured by the different lan-guages in which the models are expressed: for example, the concept of condi-tions of worth in person-centred therapy overlaps with that of super-ego in psychoanalysis and that of irrational and rational beliefs in rational emotive behaviour therapy.

Another issue is the extent to which different theoretical models may be more suitable for different clients: for example, is person-centred therapy more suited to those clients requiring nurturing and healing than more active-directive methods? A related issue is that of eclecticism. Eclecticism means drawing from different theoretical approaches. Noted psychologist Arnold Lazarus goes so far as to advocate what he terms 'techni-cal eclecticism', selecting the interventions most likely to succeed with particu-lar clients regardless of their theoretical underpinning.

A useful distinction exists between what might be termed schools of coun-selling and therapy and theoretical approaches to counselling and therapy. A theoretical approach presents a single position regarding the theory and practice of counselling and therapy. A school of counselling and therapy is a grouping of different theoretical approaches which are similar to one another in terms of certain important characteristics that distinguish them from theoretical approaches in other counselling and therapy schools. Probably the three main schools that influence contemporary individual counselling and psychotherapy practice are the psychodynamic school, the humanistic school and the cognitive-behavioural school.

Sometimes the humanistic school incorporates existential therapeutic approaches and can appropriately assume the broader title of the humanistic-existential school. This book aims to provide a repertoire of essential counselling and therapy skills that are either influenced by or directly drawn from two of the main therapeutic schools: namely, humanistic-existential and cognitive-behavioural. Theory and research intertwine in that one of the main criteria for good theory is that it sets up testable research hypotheses that, when investigated, support the theory and its application.

The issue of the contribution of research to learning counselling and therapy skills is far from simple. Research can cover a multitude of activities including creating theories and hypotheses, simple evaluations of counselling and therapy processes and outcomes, and rigorous studies that attempt to establish empir-ically supported treatments for specific psychological problems. Numerous methods exist for conducting counselling and therapy research which fall into two main categories, quantitative and qualitative.

Quantitative approaches emphasize the systematic collection and analysis of quantitative information: for example, by comparing groups of clients or by the detailed analysis of the treatment of single clients. An important distinc-tion exists between conducting one's own research and being a consumer of the research of others. In addition, just knowing about the research findings of others, for instance being conversant with an empirically supported treat-ment for a specific sexual dysfunction, provides no guarantee of being able to conduct the intervention competently oneself.

A core theoretical model, the British Association for Counselling and Psychotherapy's accredited counsel-lor training courses are required to fulfil the criterion of helping students develop as 'reflective practitioners - people who are both willing and able to reflect on all aspects of their work as counsellors, learners and members of the course'. None of the Association's nine basic elements of counsellor training focus on either conducting or on consuming research.

The reflective practitioner model insufficiently emphasizes the role of research in counsellor training and practice. Nevertheless, the goal of the reflective practitioner can be viewed as providing the grounding for a model of the role of research for counsellors. This model takes one's own coun-selling practice as its starting point. Whether they think about themselves this way or not, all counsellors are researchers continually engaged in a process of making and evaluating hypotheses in how they respond to, relate to, assess and intervene with their clients. Furthermore, supervisors are also engaged in researching the processes and outcomes of their supervisees' work.

Another model, which characterizes courses accredited by psychological societies and associations, is that of the scientist-practitioner or scientist-professional model. Placing the word 'scientist' before the word 'practitioner' indicates a model that takes academic values rather than practitioner values to be preeminent. The scientist-practitioner model assumes that counsellors and therapists require the skills of conducting as well as of consuming research. Thus in addition to such subjects as counselling theory and skills, there is a heavy emphasis on students learning statistical, computer programming, research design and conducting and evaluating research projects skills.

The fact that this heavy emphasis on all counselling and clinical psychology students need-ing to be skilled academic investigators for their future work is a research hypothesis that has never been adequately researched seems to escape most of those responsible for propounding it. Perhaps the heavy emphasis on con-ducting experimental research has more to do with power politics in acade-mic institutions and psychological societies than with the practical task of turning out skilled and humane reflective counsellors and therapists. When in training, and afterwards, only a minority of counselling and clin-ical psychology students have the talent and motivation to do genuinely cre-ative and advanced research.

Though counselling and therapy need some students trained as scientist-professionals, the reality is that most students are going to become practi-tioners. Consequently, a third model for linking research to counselling and therapy practice is that of the practitioner-researcher. The practitioner-researcher model can be viewed as building on and upgrading the reflective practitioner model. Counsellors as practitioner-researchers require the skills and motivation to evaluate their practice systematically, be it with individuals, couples or groups. Where appropriate, they can design small self-evaluative studies to this effect.

Furthermore, counsellors as practitioner-researchers can be trained in relatively straightforward service delivery programme evaluation skills. In those instances where higher-level statistical and computing expertise is required, one option is to buy it in. In addition, counsellors as practitioner-researchers require skills in order to access competently the professional and research literature regarding ther-apeutic processes and outcomes. Especially in the United States, research into therapeutic approaches is being used to establish empirically supported treatments (ESTs).

In 1993, the Society of Clinical Psychology of the American Psychological Association established a Task Force to iden-tify treatments with scientifically proven effectiveness for particular mental disorders. This task force has identified a number of effective, or probably effective, psychological treatments for disorders including depression, eating disorders, marital discord, panic disorder with and without agoraphobia, post-traumatic stress disorder, social phobia, and smoking cessation.

Therapy and Emanicipatory Praxis

Therapy and rehabilitation have a bad reputation with many disabled people. They are seen as individualising and medicalising. As such, they distract energy from challenging the main source of oppression which is the socio-political environment which discriminates against and marginalizes disabled people. Health care professionals, therapists and counsellors are often, justifiably, seen as pathologising disabled people.

The focus of the struggle, according to social model theorists, should be on transforming the built environment and social institutions so they take into account the needs of the whole population rather than the 'able-bodied/ minded' members of a community. In terms of teaching and scholarship, some have suggested that approaches with a 'remedial' endeavour, such as programmes concerned with the training of health care workers, cannot be properly considered to be 'Disability Studies' because they lack the critical social, political and cultural perspective.

The main thrust of this special issue is to challenge the disciplinary boundary between psychological and social paradigms. It argues, following a growing body of critical psycho-social literature, that conscious and unconscious experiences and social structures are inextricably intertwined. This is important when thinking about the way in which disability is both socially constructed and comes to constitute an internalised form of oppression which shapes the personal identities and relationships of both disabled and non-disabled people.

This issue begins with Stephanie Tierney's analysis of anorexia. Her paper makes an important contribution to current disability theorising by exploring the boundaries of the category 'disability'. She identifies limitations in the social model's ability to address aspects of bodily impairment and experience. There are particular kinds of implicit moral assumptions which are brought to play in popular culture in relation to 'the slimmer's disease', for example in terms of how responsibility is accorded and how mental health issues are treated. These make the condition of anorexia trivialised and those suffering from anorexia the subjects of great.hostility.

Many aspects of the experience of anorexia are similar to the experiences of disability. Yet it is also the case that many people with anorexia (as with many people with chronic illnesses or impairments) would not identify as having a disability. Beth Omansky Gordon examines the complex micro-political dynamics involved in counselling disabled students. She places emphasis on thinking about empowerment as a process. Ross Crisp takes an interpretivist perspective espousing Wendell's standpoint position for exploring the complex shared struggles and differences between people in relation to the category of disability.

Gorden and Crisp seem to be struggling, at a micro level, with the kinds of dilemmas and potential conflicts of interest which De Jong has described at the level of policy. The implications of Gorden and Crisp's argument is that what is required is that counsellors adopt a 'bi-focal' approach which involves on the one hand having a set of values. These might include beliefs about social inclusion, human rights and responsibilities, ideas about what constitutes a fulfilled life. On the other hand, counselling and therapy are client centred. Practitioners need to sustain a capacity to be in touch with where there client is in the present and what they have experienced in the past.

The client needs to experience empathy rather than an 'alternative view' in order to be helped to explore current lived and potential experiences. Thus, whilst both Beth Omansky Gordon and Ros Crisp recognise the socially constructed nature of disability, they work in such a way as to acknowledge the subjective experience of their clients even if clients see their disability in medical, psychological or spiritual terms. One key concern of this special issue is to avoid reproducing the somewhat tired binary of 'therapy-or-politics'.

Valerie Sinason's paper suggests that psychological interventions can have a political impact and questions of identity and subjectivity have political implications. Sinason's pioneering psychoanalytic work with learning disabled (mentally handicapped) clients shows that often,.behind compliant behaviour, there exists (an appropriate) rage about a hostile external world. Black slaves and their descendants in the USA learned to show their intelligence in private and adopt a 'stupid' appeasing way of talking in front of whites.

Sinason's work represents an important intervention in widening access for learning disabled (mentally handicapped) clients to psychoanalysis. Learning disabled people are more likely to be sexually abused, experience separations and generally have more disturbed developmental histories. These experiences need to be seen in the context of a society which cannot bear to tolerate certain kinds of differences. The roots of stupidity and the shame about 'not knowing' are, according to psychoanalytic writing, located in painful early experiences.

Furthermore, in a society obsessed with measuring intelligence, those institutionally designated as mentally handicapped can be profoundly unsettling to the 'normals'. Generally, in the UK, the more underprivileged a client is the more likely they are to be offered short term, practitioner centred interventions for emotional difficulties. For example, middle class professionals are more likely to receive talking treatments whilst clients who are unemployed are more likely to be offered behavioural treatments.

Learning disabled people in the UK who have 'challenging behaviour' are more likely to be subject to control and restraint than offered therapy since the aim is to 'get rid of' rather than understand their behaviour. They are seen so often as not having the 'emotional intelligence' required to make use of talking treatments. Sinason has made access to therapy possible for many leaning disabled clients and helped in training therapists at such public institutions as the Tavistock clinic in London to make their practice accessible.

Therapy can help give clients a sense of entitlement which improves self esteem and assertiveness. In this way, rather than being regulatory or normalising, therapy can help clients to become more challenging to oppressive institutions. This is not instead of changing the socio-economic, legal and cultural framework which produces disability, but part of changing that context.

There are very important and justified criticisms of the theories and practices of professionals whose aim is to offer counselling to disabled people. Therapists need a political education to overcome their own conscious and unconscious assumptions and prejudices about certain forms of difference. Psychological writing on disability is often reductive, treating disability not as a complex life experience which needs to be understood in the context of relationships, but rather as a purely individual personal tragedy which the disabled person needs to adjust to and come to terms with. Having an understanding of the kinds of structures and experiences which construct identities in relation to disability is central to creating an inclusive counselling/therapeutic practice.

All too often therapy, and particularly psychoanalytic psychotherapy, is wrongly seen as being necessarily a conservative and oppressive force which focuses back on the individual. This is particularly the accusation levelled at psychoanalytic work. Psychotherapy /analysis is a profoundly ethical practice. Self-esteem is both personal and socio-cultural. Axel Honneth shows that self-respect and self-esteem are both personal and political demands. This special issue attempts to grapple with ways of fostering a bi-focal vision which takes in an understanding of both macro structures and relations and subjective and interpersonal experience of disability.

Feminist Therapy

Many women are actually seeking special favors, such as hiring policies that favor them over men, under the guise of asking for "equality." New approaches to women's psychological health have emerged in the wake of the revitalized Women's Movement. Since 1970, we have achieved public recognition of the separate forces that impact on women and men in Western societies.

New scholarship and research on the psychology of women introduced the "second sex" into the medical and psychological literature and brought the life span issues of women into sharper focus. The social construction of gender relocates women's problems from individual and internal to societal and external. The feminist construction of gender redefines the nature of women's and men's relationships in terms of the expression and maintenance of power.

The multicultural construction of gender identifies the intersects of gender, ethnicity, socioeconomic class (SES), and sexual orientation that shape our personal and social identities. The changes that have transpired in the past 30 years hold enormous implications for the ways in which psychological practice with women takes place.

Emergent client populations were "discovered" where problems were invisible and never believed to exist. The challenges of these new client populations stimulated the development of theories, research, and procedures to address their concerns. The combined efforts of women's groups in both the lay and professional communities have resulted in new agendas for women's mental health.

The foundation for these agendas is rooted in the history and expression of feminism, which nurtures and promotes the goal of equality in all aspects of women's and men's lives, and among diverse groups of people. As emergent ideologies challenged traditional views, the field of psychology began to expand in new directions. The result of this expansion has been a wealth of new research and knowledge about women and men, revised theories to explain and account for psychological development, and a demand for creative applications to prevent and remediate human problems.

The fledgling discipline of the Psychology of Women was established, providing the foundation for an applied science dedicated to counseling and therapy with women. In the field of mental health, the consideration of sex, gender, and cultural diversity in the prevalence, etiology, diagnosis, and treatment of a range of human problems was conspicuously absent until recently.

Two epidemiological surveys of community samples sponsored by the National Institute of Mental Health (NIMH) revealed that a high proportion of individuals with signs of depression, anxiety, panic, simple phobia, and agoraphobia are women, whereas men are overrepresented in the categories of substance abuse and antisocial behaviors. According to these surveys, in the United States, overall health and community mental health utilization rates are higher for women than for men.

Women are prescribed a disproportionate share of psychoactive drugs, many of which have deleterious or unknown side effects. Dissatisfaction with existing theories, knowledge base, and treatment approaches motivated a call for change. In response to their growing awareness of personal dissatisfaction and unexplained malaise, groups of women began to congregate to discuss their life situations. In sharing experiences of restricted and stereotyped expectations for how they should conduct their lives, they discovered that their problems were voiced and mirrored by others.

The growing awareness of asymmetrical gender expectations and widespread discrimination and injustice for women resulted in the conclusion that " the personal is political." Consciousnessraising groups were therapeutic for many and were instrumental in the early call for change in the sexist and oppressive social structures that characterized a patriarchal, or male dominated, society. Consciousness-raising groups were directed toward accomplishing social change rather than healing personal wounds.

The impetus for seeking alternative approaches to women's well-being came from many directions, as researchers and clinicians voiced their concerns. Expression of these concerns covered a broad range of issues that addressed both the deficits in our psychological knowledge about women and the problems that existed with current intervention models and practices in the mental health field.

The emergence of a specialty area in counseling and psychotherapy with women was predicated on four factors that supported its development:

1. The Psychology of Women became a reality, providing a substantial body of theory and knowledge about the diverse biological, cultural, and psychological characteristics of women.
2. New client populations emerged whose needs for intervention and treatment were not addressed by current traditional approaches to therapy.
3. Revised models of women's mental health and well-being integrated new information about women and proposed innovative goals for women's empowerment.
4. Alternative counseling models were developed that addressed the unique characteristics and goals of underserved populations.

In the wake of these developments, training programs in the specialty of counseling and psychotherapy with women were initiated and implemented. Each of these factors further in terms of their contributions to the specialty of counseling and psychotherapy with women. Counseling has been applied historically to interventions that assist clients in understanding and resolving ongoing problems in living. As such, counseling tends to focus on positive aspects of psychological health and well-being. Psychotherapy, in contrast, has been applied traditionally to medical or illness models that locate problems in persons and that aim to reduce or "cure" pathology in patients.

The first requirement for the development of a specialty area is the accumulation of a body of knowledge that serves as a database for theory, research, and applications to practice. Four major outcomes of innovative research on women and gender include:

1. New information about women and the diversity of their lives in contemporary society.
2. Revised views of sex, gender, gender roles, and gender-related behavior.
3. Diversity and multicultural perspectives.
4. Feminist psychology, feminist theory, and implications for training and practice.

Early research related to the psychology of women focused on a search for sex-related differences, or those that might be found between girls and boys, women and men. In exhaustive searches of the literature published between 1967 and 1982, Mary Roth Walsh found over 13,000 citations related to the psychology of women. Kay Deaux reported 18,000 citations that covered sex-related differences and sex roles. Since then, the psychological literature on women and gender has increased geometrically as the burgeoning research fills both old and new journals. In the early publications, attention centered on characteristics assumed to differentiate the sexes, such as self- esteem, intellectual abilities, achievement variables, career development, interpersonal relationships, aggression, dominance, and verbal and nonverbal behavior.

Feminist psychology encouraged moving research on women out of the laboratory to look at the meaningful contexts of their lives. This research brought, new information about women in relation to the roles they occupy in Western societies (e.g., daughter, wife, lover, partner, mother, worker), the discriminatory practices that restrict their opportunities in almost all societies (e.g., in education, employment, politics, public life), the victimization and violence they experience in most societies (e.g., incest, rape, sexual harassment, physical battering), the diverse groups with which they affiliate (e.g., women of color and differing subcultures, lesbians, older women, disabled), and their psychological processes (e.g., well-being, self-esteem, stress, anger, depression, anxiety).

As women's experiences are explored in the context of their diverse lives, innovative research strategies and approaches have been developed to address the complex questions that were not previously considered. The illumination of women's lives in context also leads to ask creatively about how the sum and interaction among these experiences frame our sense of personal and social identity.

Gender-Related Behavior

Although the call for change rallied around the issues that faced contemporary women, it soon became clear that women's concerns could be reinterpreted in the broader context of gender. That is, researchers in the field hypothesized that behaviors and attitudes previously believed to be determined by sex (female or male) were socially and situationally created rather than intrinsic to the individual. Some research provided evidence that women's and men's behaviors could be understood in the context of the status inequalities between the two sexes as well as between members of dominant and subordinate subcultures in the United States.

Thus, many of the obtained gender-related behaviors could be interpreted as evidence of unequal power relations between socially defined groups. For many professionals in the field, gender becomes the major issue in working with women. "The social construction of gender plays a major role in the definition and diagnosis of illness, timing and expression of symptoms, treatment strategies, and theoretical explanations. Thus, mental illness is as much a social as a personal event".

Only recently have there been attempts to integrate these perspectives in counseling and therapy with women. Diversity encompasses all aspects of a person's social realities: gender, culture, ethnicity and national origin, immigration and acculturation status, sexual and affectional orientation, age, education, socioeconomic status (SES), physical characteristics and abilities, intellectual abilities, and religious affiliation. The consideration of diversity in counseling and therapy is important for two major reasons: First, it is critical for the therapist to understand and be responsive to the cultural context and personal meanings of the client's behavior and her current concerns. Second, the social locations by which she identifies herself and is identified by others provide opportunities for her to experience both pride and oppression. Clients may gain self-esteem and personal empowerment by identifying with groups they view as socially valued. But many of these socially identified groups are culturally stigmatized by negative attitudes, stereotyped beliefs, and active discrimination; these are the conditions that lead to oppression.

Although racism is a toxic element in most societies that creates stigma and oppression for individuals in socially identified groups, biologists and anthropologists tell us that "race" is also a socially constructed category. As such, it does not represent the reality of genetic difference but rather, ref lects the power of dominant social groups to define who is "in" and who is "out." Because the concept of race highlights presumed differences that are immutable, we prefer to speak of ethnicity, as inclusive of both "race" and the cultural and language frameworks that influence how people construct meanings and lifestyles. But because physical features and skin color also provide stimuli for inferring "race," it is also important to speak of racism in terms of the ways in which dominant cultures stigmatize and discriminate against those whom it defines as racially different or "inferior."

As women from non-White groups voiced their concern about their marginal status and invisibility in feminist psychology. A broad definition of multiculturalism presents it as "a philosophy that affords the development of f lexibility and diversity of orientations to life and for the development of pluralistic identities". Hope Landrine proposed a multicultural feminist psychology that incorporates the contextual meanings of behavior for all cultures. By culture, mean shared learned behaviors and values of a particular group that are transmitted across generations. Culture includes external components such as institutions, language, and visible artifacts, social norms and social roles (rules and expectations for behavior), and internal components such as attitudes, values, world views, and ways of thinking about the self in relation to the collective.

According to Helen Markus and her associates, "Communities, societies, and cultural contexts provide the interpretive frameworks-including images, concepts, and narratives, as well as the means, practices, and patterns of behavior-by which people make sense and organize their actions". Derald Sue and David Sue called for a multicultural counseling model that places cultural identity at the center. Their multicultural approach counteracts the racial and ethnic biases encountered by people of color. These biases tend to define people of color as the "problem," identifying their differences as due to genetic deficiency (they are intellectually inferior), cultural deficiency (they are culturally deprived), and pathology (they are abnormal or deviant).

Instead of problematizing minority groups, the multicultural model is based on the assumption of difference rather than deviance, viewing cultural and ethnic experiences as strengths that are valuable to both the person and society. In a broader view of multicultural counseling, Leroy Baruth and Lee Manning include differences in culture, world views, and the nature of reality as well as the variables of gender, sexual orientation, and life stage. Sex differences in performance, such as in spatial relations, are attributed to the selective effects of male androgens on the right cerebral hemisphere. In both examples, gendered patterns of behavior are assumed to result from endogenous or biological variables that ref lect " true" sex differences. Based on her examination of extensive data, Ruth Bleier, a biologist, concluded that there is no firm evidence for a biological basis of behavioral differences between females and males.

Feminist Psychology

Research and scholarship in the psychology of women is not necessarily feminist. There is a great deal of overlap and the major scholarly journal, the Psychology of Women Quarterly, is feminist in its goals, procedures, and content. The range of belief systems attached to the term feminist is broad. Over 20 years ago, Webster's New World Dictionary (1978) defined feminism as (a) "The principle that women should have political, economic, and social rights equal to those of men," and (b) "the movement to win such rights for women". Thus, the dictionary definition included an appeal to social justice and advocacy for social change.

From a broader theoretical perspective, feminist theories have addressed the question of how to explain the inequality between women and men in almost all cultures and across all historical times, and how this injustice should be remedied. The Liberal feminist viewpoint targets inequalities in legal, political, and educational arrangements and promotes laws to redress inequities in opportunity for education and employment. In contrast, the Cultural feminist addresses the male-dominated culture that devalues women's relational qualities and seeks to empower women by celebrating the unique qualities of women, viewing them as caring, intimate, cooperative, and connected to others. These qualities are valued and become the major source of power and liberation.

From a Radical feminist approach, however, women's oppression is rooted in patriarchy, or the unequal allocation of power in society to men. The source of women's oppression lies in institutional male dominance and control of all aspects of women's lives. The identification of patriarchy as a system of male privilege leads to solutions that go beyond "equal pay for equal work," and leads logically to requirements for activism to achieve social and institutional change.

Women of Color feminism identifies institutional racism as the major source of women's oppression. Thus, patriarchy, a system of male domination, is not the only source of oppression; both White women and men of color can be oppressors as well as being the oppressed. Social change must come through acknowledging and reducing White privilege, honoring the values and culture of oppressed minority groups, and eliminating both institutional racism and sexism.

Finally, Lesbian feminism identifies both patriarchy and heterosexism as bases for the oppression of women. The assumption that heterosexuality is "normal" frames alternate sexualities and lifestyles as deviant and undesirable, leading to discrimination, exclusion from public life, and restricted civil rights of women who love and live with other women. One proposed solution to challenging heterosexism, albeit not the only one, has been to advocate legislative action toward equality for sexual minorities under the law. As another solution, the promotion of "gay pride" has empowered many in this community to reject social bias and discrimination and to affirm their self-esteem.

The range of definitions and theories about feminism leads to conclude that feminism, as a social and political movement, is broad and multifaceted. It is clear that many differing attitudes and values are associated with being a feminist, but all roads lead to a simple conclusion: Equality of opportunity, respect, and fair treatment for all persons is essential.

The advances of the Psychology of Women in terms of theory and knowledge provide exciting implications for training programs in counseling and psychotherapy. An effective program for training counselors for women incorporates a research component that avoids gender and multicultural bias in method and content, and that explores the diverse lives of both women and men. The program also includes a feminist analysis of client issues and careful supervision to provide constructive feedback to the therapist. We believe that without such awareness, you are likely to impose your stereotypes on your clients. In doing so, you may unwittingly support them in "adjusting" to the status quo and in remaining in subordinate life positions.

Dramatic changes in the formation and maintenance of family roles in the past 20 years have lead to a shift in many women's lifestyles, in the situations they face, and in the problems with which they cope. In particular, women are remaining single more frequently and for longer periods of time, finding partners or marrying later, having fewer children, entering the paid labor force at an unprecedented rate, developing new career paths, separating and divorcing more often, coping with single parenting and stepparenting, reentering higher education at later ages, experiencing interrupted careers and employment paths, and repartnering or remarrying.

They are growing older and living longer, and may find themselves "sandwiched" between growing children and elderly parents, or living alone. New definitions of "family" have encouraged marginalized groups such as lesbian and bisexual women to confront their relationship needs more openly. Each of these life events may present situational coping problems and issues for which women seek help.

The increase of women in the paid labor force confronts them with a host of new issues: managing multiple roles, negotiating dual-career and egalitarian relationships, coping with role conflict (work-family balance) and role strain (work-family stress), nontraditional career development and change, employment discrimination, pay equity, professional isolation, sexual harassment, management and leadership training, assertiveness concerns, workforce reentry, and retirement.

The prevalence of singleness and high divorce rates opens up issues of finding new relationships, establishing sexual satisfaction, developing social support networks, divorce counseling, child custody and maintenance decisions, managing stepchildren and reconstituted families, and coping with financial stress and loneliness.

Certain syndromes have increased in reported frequency as society places continuing demands on women to conform to gender-role standards, and as women are becoming concerned with the care and maintenance of their bodies. There is a rising prevalence of girls and women concerned with body image and weight control, as evidenced by eating disturbances such as anorexia, bulimia, and obesity. Women also seek psychological help in dealing with medical and physical concerns:

AIDS, mastectomy, menstrual-related distress, reproductive issues including pregnancy, unplanned pregnancy and infertility, and problems concerning the abuse of addictive substances such as alcohol and prescription drugs.

Women in high-risk groups are those with issues that are compounded by exclusion and discrimination as a result of experiences of racism, ageism, homophobia, immigration, and poverty. Women from high-risk groups have been reluctant to seek help from the mental health community, partly because they anticipate and frequently experience a reenactment of societal discrimination in psychotherapy. As new multicultural approaches to counseling and therapy are developed and practiced, more of these women are encouraged to seek help in dealing with their particular concerns.

The emergence of multiple and complex lifespan issues for women in contemporary Western societies provides a sufficient rationale for the development of new approaches for addressing these issues. The implications of diverse client populations for both research and practice are evident.

Psychological Practices

The development of feminist principles and procedures in counseling stretches from the early beginnings of consciousness-raising groups to the 1982 establishment of the Feminist Therapy Institute for advanced psychotherapists. There are four essential principles of feminist practice:

1. *Attention to the diversity of women's personal and social identities*: The intersects of women's multiple identities, whether consciously experienced or unaware, are explored and examined for their inf luences on client expectations and behaviors, and on their experiences of privilege or oppression.

2. *A consciousness-raising approach*: Clients are helped to differentiate between the politics of the sexist, racist, or homophobic societal structures that inf luence their lives and those problems over which they have realistic control. Intrapsychic causation for problems in living is supplanted by exploration of gender-role messages mediated by their culture, societal expectations, and institutionalized sexism, racism, or homophobia.

3. *An egalitarian relationship between client and therapist*: The client is encouraged to set personal goals and trust her own experience and judgment. Power differentials between client and therapist are minimized.

4. A woman-valuing and self-validating process. Communal qualities of interdependence, concern for others, emotional expression, and cooperation are valued and honored. Women are encouraged to identify their strengths, to value and nurture themselves, and to bond with other women. Language forms that devalue women are reframed from weakness to strengths (e.g., terms such as enmeshed and fused may be reframed as caring, concerned, and nurturing).

Empowerment model of Counselling

An empowerment model of counseling that incorporates and expands on the theoretical perspectives and principles described earlier. Empowerment is a broad goal of feminist intervention that enables individuals, families, and communities to exert influence over the personal, interpersonal, and institutional factors that impact their health and well-being . The overall goals of personal and social empowerment emphasize client strengths and resilience in coping with past, current, and future trauma and stress.

Power has been defined in many ways and is a term that communicates both positive and negative meanings. Power hierarchies can exist at many levels: individual, interpersonal, organizational, and societal. At a more societal level, Carolyn Sherif described power as control over social institutions and their various resources, enabling the power holder to establish rules, initiate action, make decisions, and impose rewards and punishments on others. Although power is typically associated with gender, males holding more than females in most societies, power also interacts with other socially defined groups.

For the dominant group, oppression can be justified by defining subordinate groups as different or inferior, and thus they can be seen as less in need or less deserving of these resources. Oppression creates a toxic environment for subordinate groups that may result in illness and alienation. For example, by constructing the "true" nature of women as passive, nurturant, indecisive, and emotional, they become clearly more suited than men for household duties, child care, and other care, and less suited for business or organizational leadership. Since both women and ethnocultural minority groups are subordinate in Western societies, empowerment may enable them to reclaim the asymmetry in access to valued resources.

Empowerment is conceptualized in two ways in the context of therapy. First, clients are empowered in dealing with their life situations through achieving skills and flexibility in problem solution, and developing a full range of interpersonal and life skills. They learn to identify and cherish their personal strengths and assets as well as recognize their responsibility for change. Cultural and personal identities are explored for their contributions to client concerns and for their relevance in strengthening personal and cultural pride. Second, empowerment encourages women to identify and challenge the external conditions of their lives that devalue and subordinate them as women or as members of minority groups, and that deny them equality of opportunity and access to valued social, economic, and institutional resources-those sources of reward, sustenance, support, or opportunity that are identified as important and meaningful by each group or individual.

Feminist approaches to empowerment thus incorporate both internal and external contributions to personal distress and well-being, and assist women to discriminate between them. This discrimination functions to free them from feelings of being different, deficient, "crazy," or out of control; it replaces their sense of powerlessness with strength and pride in their ability to cope with current and future challenges. These new feelings and skills lead to increasing resilience in coping with stress and adversity. Resilience and thriving are new ways to look at the mental health outcomes of feminist therapy.

Empowerment is assumed to lead to resilience through supporting the knowledge and skills that facilitate effective coping with future situational inequities, discrimination, exclusion, and interpersonal stress. The resilient person is able to respond to increased stress and negative life events with effective coping skills that enable her to maintain her sense of well-being and effective functioning. These may be skills and attitudes that are learned early in life, capabilities acquired through survival following aversive events, or skills developed through an affirmative and empowering therapy experience. We think of empowerment and resilience as more than the absence of pathology.

Strategies of Feminist Psychology

As we have seen, the tenets of feminist counseling and therapy cut across diverse theories and specific techniques. Feminist therapists endorse a range of theoretical views and employ many different kinds of strategies and specific interventions. We are personally committed to two different, but not incompatible, theoretical views: cognitivebehavioral, and psychodrama. Each of us has adapted a basic theoretical orientation and techniques to render it compatible with EFT principles and procedures.

Some theories may be more conducive to this transformation process than others, depending on the extent to which they endorse gender-biased or ethnocentric concepts or procedures. Ethnocentric concepts assume that the language and constructs that apply to one group are universal across all groups. Across various theories, however, some techniques are used commonly by most feminist therapists.

Strategies that may be common to most feminist approaches include gender-role analysis, power analysis, and demystifying methods. In gender-role analysis, clients are helped to identify how societal structures and expectations related to traditional gender arrangements have influenced their lives. In demystification, clients are provided with information about therapeutic procedures and the process of change, and with the tools for evaluating and monitoring their own progress. While demystification is not unique to feminist approaches, it is used strategically as a means of reducing the power differential between client and therapist and thus empowering the client.

More recently, multicultural perspectives have emphasized the importance of a cultural analysis, recognizing that psychological intervention always occurs in a cultural context. Clients are encouraged to explore their personal and social identities, and how their assimilation of the dominant or external culture matches or conflicts with their internally generated cultural messages and values. In the context of therapy, cultural differences across the three-way interaction among client, therapist, and the intervention setting may produce tensions and misunderstandings.

Psychological Interventions

Psychological interventions (talking treatments) provide an important contribution to the treatment of anxiety and depression in the community. They are popular with service users as reliance on drug treatment is reduced and in terms of improving people's mental health. In October 2001 the Scottish Executive launched the Framework for Mental Health Services in Scotland. This lays out the core service elements for services offering psychological interventions. An important building block in developing this supplement to the 1997 Framework was work undertaken as part of the Scottish Executive funded initiative for the expansion and improvement of local Psychological interventions.

The Framework draws on a growing evidence base for psychological interventions and was informed by recent guidelines produced by the Department of Health in England supporting the use of psychological interventions particularly for those with anxiety and/or depression. Annex A is a timely addition to the range of mental health policy and practice guidance directed at local health and social care agencies.

It fits with the renewed emphasis on mental health and well being and the aspiration to achieve improvement in the mental health of the people of Scotland. It recognises Local Health Care Co-operatives (LHCCs) as essential partners in the provision of mental health services and acknowledges the increasing number and diversity of professions and agencies (statutory and voluntary) offering psychosocial interventions locally. Further, its provides a means of addressing timely access to psychological interventions by reviewing and where necessary redesigning the way in which such interventions are organised and delivered.

The key aim was to achieve optimum outcomes for people who require psychological interventions by improving access routes into services, by achieving better targeting of resources and by improving and sustaining the training and skills base of psychosocial interventions practitioners.

The role of the Scottish Development Centre was to support services and agencies in developing care processes that ensured access to and delivery of psychological therapeutic interventions. Tackling delays and improving access to psychological interventions is not only about addressing limited resources but may also be indicators of system malfunctions.

GPs are usually the main gatekeepers to psychological interventions. Without a clear understanding of who is providing what and for whom, it is difficult for them to determine where to refer and whether services and skills are being effectively deployed to meet the full spectrum of needs for psychological interventions.

Statutory services often support self-referrals to voluntary agencies for psychological interventions rather than make direct referrals. The pilots uncovered a general lack of confidence from statutory staff about the effectiveness, quality and accountability of voluntary organisations, some of which were established for up to 20 years. This lack of confidence may reflect poor communication between the statutory and voluntary organisations and if so represents a missed opportunity for referrers, providers and service users and carers.

Effectiveness and accountability are essential to voluntary agencies as part of the process of securing renewal of their contracts with statutory services to whom they are directly accountable. Supervision, service evaluation and contract monitoring are regular activities in the voluntary sector. It is important that the voluntary sector is able to demonstrate to health colleagues the processes they have in place to supervise, monitor and evaluate their quality of care.

The different services involved in providing psychological interventions are frequently over compartmentalised, causing a fragmented system. Often there is a lack of knowledge and understanding, respect and value for different approaches amongst different professionals. This is particularly acute between statutory and voluntary agencies. Effective developments take steps to address these issues.

Modern, evidence based psychological interventions should be provided via multiple access points which are organised systematically in a tiered, needs based system. Creating a tiered approach between primary and secondary care involves establishing agreed responsibilities regarding the levels of mental health need each service caters for. This is particularly relevant between primary and secondary care to reduce the unnecessary referrals to already overloaded specialist services.

Specialist services can be used more effectively to provide consultation, advice and supervision to primary care and other providers catering for those with mild to moderate psychological needs. Communicating service availability and access to referrers and public Information about availability of psychological interventions and expectations of treatment or intervention is rarely available from the referrer at referral.

General practitioners need guidance on the best forms of management at the referral stage and providing choice for users should be a primary aim of communicating information about services and what they offer. Services should be organised so that clients and referrers can access information about them in a methodical way.

The Therapeutic Community Treatment Model

This section analyses the strengths and weaknesses of the therapeutic approach, known as the therapeutic community (TC) model, described in the above motion. The therapeutic community (TC) can be understood as both a model and a treatment approach for people with substance abuse and related problems. In its current incarnation, two main types of TCs can be identified. The first, dating back to the 1940s, concerns itself with the treatment of psychiatric patients within and outside of hospital settings.

The term, 'therapeutic community' was initially used to describe this type of TC. The second type of TC is abstinence-based, and aims to treat and rehabilitate persons with addictions and related problems. This second type of TC, which emerged in North America in the 1960s. The TC for the treatment of addictions is defined as follows:

> "A therapeutic community is a drug-free environment in which people with addictive (and other) problems live together in an organized and structured way in order to promote change and make possible a drug-free life in the outside society. The therapeutic community forms a miniature society in which residents, and staff in the role of facilitators, fulfil distinctive roles and adhere to clear

rules, all designed to promote the transitional process of the residents".

Recent years have seen TCs adapt to serve the particular needs of a number of 'special populations' including adolescents, HIV positive and AIDS clients, homeless men and women, mothers and children, mentally ill chemical abusers and methadone clients. Even as they adapt and diversify, a number of 'essential elements' of the therapeutic community can be identified.

The physical environment

TCs can be found in a variety of settings including residential neighbourhoods and suburbs, industrial sites, and rural settings. However a number of facilities are found in inner-city areas, some near drug-affected urban neighbourhoods. TCs operate in purpose-built structures, as well as a range of converted buildings such as tenement housing, hotels, schools, churches or nursing homes. The size, grounds and design of facilities also vary, but are generally adapted to the types of educational and vocational training offered by the TC. The residential capacity of a TC program commonly ranges from 50 - 150 residents. An 'ideal' size is often described to be in the range of 80 - 120 residents, although exceptions include Delancey Street which has a residential capacity of approximately 450 - 500 beds.

Therapeutic communities are not locked facilities but 'semi-closed' environments where residents choose voluntarily to live for a period of 3 to 24 months, and in some cases, longer. Although strict limits are placed on residents' comings and goings, residents who comply with all house rules and program requirements may gradually earn privileges to leave the facility through day, overnight or weekend passes, particularly to visit parents, partners or children. An exception is found in the case of those residents mandated by the court to a certain length of stay in a TC. Court mandated residents who leave the facility without permission may have warrants issued for their arrest.

The key interior spaces in a TC consist of areas where the operational, educational, and therapeutic activities of the program are held. Common spaces include lounges, seminar rooms, classrooms, training facilities, the dining room, and kitchen. Private spaces include administrative offices and conference rooms. Sleeping quarters are often dormitory style, segregated by gender, and sometimes by factors such as age or stage in the program. Some TCs have on-site medical and dental offices.

Other hallmark features of the physical environment of the TC include the front desk, where all traffic in and out of the facility is monitored, and structure boards and charts which provide an 'up-to-the-hour' visual picture of the status and location of each resident in or out of the facility, often organized around the daily schedule and activities in the TC.

Staffing

TCs are often staffed by a carefully chosen group of professionals who receive training in the specifics of the TC model. Experts suggest that program staff should comprise a mix of self-help recovered professionals and other traditional professionals (e.g. nurses, physicians, lawyers, case workers, counsellors) who must be integrated through therapeutic community-grounded training. An average resident to staff ratio was cited as approximately 15:1, with smaller ratios found in TCs that serve a higher proportion of adolescent and other special needs populations.

The social environment: peer dynamic and hierarchical structure

One of the characteristics that often distinguishes the therapeutic community from other treatment approaches is the use of the peer community to "facilitate social and psychological change in individuals". This means that the community itself is understood to form an integral part of the therapeutic approach to recovery. The assumption is that individuals are impacted most profoundly when they meet and surpass community expectations.

As part of daily life in the TC, residents observe and monitor each other's participation and roles in the community. In this way, the peer dynamic is argued to be a persuasive influence in residents' desire to become more responsible and accountable, which then extends from the individual, to peers, and finally the entire community. The highly structured environment of a TC can be seen in both the physical and social organization of the community. A TC generally consists of several work and training departments such as the kitchen, maintenance, administration, etc. Each department has specific responsibilities and internal hierarchy, with the departments themselves making up an overall hierarchical order (Broekaert 2001: 34). Each resident begins at the 'bottom' of the hierarchy (sweeping floors or cleaning bathrooms, for example), and works his or her way up through the ranks of more desirable jobs and departments. Sleeping quarters can also be arranged by seniority status, with more long-staying residents earning rooms with fewer roommates, or in some cases, private rooms.

Resident profile and special populations

Most residents of TCs are considered to have hit 'rock bottom' whether they voluntarily enter a community or arrive through the criminal justice system. Many residents have been drug addicted for years and have a history of criminal activity or other legal problems. Other common factors include multi-generational poverty and homelessness. The typical gender breakdown is approximately ¾ male and ¼ female, with many women residents having given up custody of children.Although many residents arrive with a host of health related problems, most TCs stipulate that residents must be healthy enough to undertake physical labour and participate in training programs and other group-related activities.

Potential residents are generally deemed inadmissible in the case of a history of kidnapping, rape, arson, child molestation, suicide attempts, violence or serious mental illness. Unless a TC is specifically designed to accommodate a youth population, the age of residents can range from 18 - 68, with an average range being between approximately 28 - 40. TCs designed for a youth population are generally smaller in size, often have a much lower staff to resident ratio, and are widely perceived to bring specific challenges because of the population they serve.

The screening and intake process for TC residents is rigorous, typically involving an initial visit or phone call, admission to a waiting list, an orientation process, one or more intake interviews, medical, legal and psychological assessments, and consent to treatment. A thorough intake process is considered to be particularly critical in light of the high rate of drop-out which commonly reaches 50% within the first 30 days.

The treatment process: therapy, education and training

The elements of treatment at the TC typically include substance abuse treatment, education (General Equivalency Diploma or, in some cases, university courses), primary medical and dental care, vocational skills training (e.g. culinary arts, carpentry, general maintenance, mechanical systems, general contracting, computer skills, or substance abuse counselling), on- and off-site job placement, and in rare cases, on-site resident-run businesses. Other supports include legal services, advocacy, and life skills counselling.

In some TCs, support groups are offered to groups based on ethnicity, sexual orientation, age and health status. Although residents may gradually earn the privilege of leaving the TC to attend a religious institution of their choice, there is no formal religious component to treatment, education or training. In fact, experts caution against the introduction of religion as an aspect of daily life in the TC.

The daily regimen

Residents can expect a highly structured and demanding daily regimen within the TC. The typical day includes a 6:30 or 7:00 AM wake-up call, morning and evening house meetings, job functions, therapeutic groups, life skill seminars, vocational training sessions, some personal time, recreation, and individual counselling when necessary. Weekend schedules are somewhat less demanding. Structure and routine are integral to the daily regimen.

Re-integrating into the community

An important part of the TC approach involves preparing the resident for re-integration, or 're-entry,' into the wider society. Some TCs insist that no resident leaves the program without a full-time job including benefits, a place to live and a support network. Family reunification is often incorporated into re-entry. The underlying philosophy is that re-entry is a transitional process over time requiring the development of a host of coping skills and supports. One of the supports most commonly identified as essential to resident success once they leave the TC is transitional housing and affordable longer-term housing for TC 'graduates.'

In New York, the Center for Therapeutic Community Research (CTCR), are not treatment facilities. While the CTCR is an internationally renowned centre for research on the Therapeutic Community model. The Center for Therapeutic Community Research (CTCR) conducts systematic research on refining techniques and improving the effectiveness of treatment. In addition, it focuses on modifying the unique therapeutic community approach to special populations and settings such as mentally ill chemical abusers (MICAs) in community residences, adolescent substance abusers in residential TCs, and criminal offenders in corrections facilities. The CTCR is redefining an assessment instrument for measuring readiness for treatment, developing a system for classifying TC programs, and establishing a national TC database.

In recent years, that community has expanded. Walden House is centered in the San Francisco Bay Area, yet delivers services throughout California. Based on the therapeutic community (TC) model of treatment, the program emphasizes self-help and peer support in a highly structured, humanistic environment. Services are available in a day treatment setting or variable length residential settings depending on each client's unique needs.

From a programmatic perspective, the Therapeutic Community (TC) treatment model is characterized by a number of distinct elements. Among the most significant elements are (1) the therapeutic approach itself, (2) staffing issues, and (3) issues relating to "success rates" and outcomes. One of the most distinctive components of the TC treatment model is the therapeutic approach itself. Although variation exists between various TCs, the therapeutic approach is typically based on concrete program stages distinguished by the attainment of specific goals.

The process of moving through program stages is monitored not only by TC staff, but also by community of residents themselves, thus creating the 'community peer dynamic' described as essential to the TCs philosophy and operation. The end points of each program stage are well marked in terms of expected behaviour and attitudes. An example of a typical phased TC treatment model can be found in the following brief summaries.

The first phase of a TC program can be described as the induction stage. Once the intake process of interviews and assessments is complete, new arrivals to the TC are often housed in rooms with six to eight bunkmates.Each room typically has a room 18 leader who is responsible for the orientation of the new resident to the rules and expectations of the TC. The new resident joins a daily encounter group made up of peers and professional counsellors. It is believed that the group serves the purpose of "challenging and overcoming negative behaviours."

Work is often identified as one of the central components of the therapeutic approach. As such, job assignments or "functions" begin immediately for new residents, usually with basic housekeeping or maintenance chores. The work-centred approach is intended to serve multiple purposes. First, by beginning with general maintenance work, the resident acquires knowledge of the facility's physical layout and organizational structure. Second, daily work is believed to instil an ethic of discipline and hard work that is desirable according to the TC treatment model. Third, putting new residents to work immediately reinforces the broader nature of the TC as a structured, merit-based program, where residents earn privileges and seniority by complying with all rules and behavioural expectations.

In this case, the implied goal for the new resident is to move up a strict hierarchy of jobs and departments to more desirable positions. Lastly, the work is often physically demanding, leaving residents physically tired at the end of the day so that they have no time to think about leaving and returning to their previous lifestyle. Evenings are usually spent in "encounter groups,"educational training groups or other study groups. Progression from phase one to phase two is be made on the recommendation of staff members and, to a lesser extent, the broader peer group, and is typically judged on the basis of the individual resident's attitude, work competence and peer relations.

In Phase two the resident is expected to take on more responsibility for the welfare of others, particularly newcomers. At this stage, he or she is normally introduced to three vocational training areas. Training takes place during the daytime hours, with expected study time in the evening. Residents typically begin courses to improve literacy, develop computer skills and achieve a General Equivalency Diploma (GED).

Residents are also typically expected to continue with their encounter groups, with the goal of adopting positive beliefs and attitudes toward themselves and others. By the end of phase two, residents are normally expected to have completed their GED, choose one vocation training area in which to specialize, participate in encounter groups, deal with more daily responsibility, and adhere to the rules and regulations of the facility.

Entry into phase three normally begins when the resident has applied for, and has been accepted to train in a vocational area on a full-time basis, with the intention of completing a certificate in the program or trade, and finding related work outside of the facility after leaving. Residents may be reimbursed nominally for their vocational work. The money is saved so they will have money to begin their new lives once they exit the program. Staff typically ensure that residents have dealt with all outstanding legal issues (e.g. warrants, custody disputes) that may have arisen prior to entry into the program.

During this phase, residents may be encouraged to attend social activities outside of the facility accompanied by other members, as well as re-establish contact with their families of origin. A family reunification program is sometimes established. At this point residents typically share accommodations and bathrooms with a smaller number of residents in a more home like setting. It is believed that by this phase, residents have acquired skills and coping abilities to allow them to "re-enter" society.

These skills often include a GED, vocational training, computer literacy, and relationship and coping skills. If any money has been saved for the resident, these funds will be released with the expectation that a bank account will be opened for living expenses.

Although San Francisco's Delancey Street shares many essential characteristics of a TC, it does not formally identify itself as such. One of the most distinctive features of Delancey that sets it apart as an exception to the way most TCs are designed and run, is its entrepreneurial focus. While most TCs offer vocational training and apprenticeship as an aspect of the program, Delancey operates a number of on-site businesses that are run by residents, thereby providing "on the job" experience and training (without pay). Delancey Street's businesses include a moving company, a restaurant, a catering business, a print and copy shop and paratransit services.

Unlike other TCs, where funding is drawn from a number of public and private sources, Delancey Street accepts no government funds. Instead, the Delancey Street businesses generate the majority of revenue to run the facility. The entrepreneurial focus of Delancey Street is cited by leading experts on TCs as a rare exception. Another, perhaps more contentious feature that sets Delancey Street apart from most other TCs, is the fact that it operates with no professional staff, with residents performing all functions in the facility including therapeutic aspects of treatment.

Unlike the majority of other TCs, Delancey Street residents can choose to live at the facility indefinitely.

Consequently, long-term residents often take on job functions that would be performed by professional staff in other programs. The no-staff model is controversial, with experts and operators holding varying opinions on the desirability of such an approach.

One particular accreditation body whose expertise is often sought by TCs is the Commission on Accreditation of Rehabilitation Facilities (CARF). CARF is an independent, not-for-profit organization that has accredited more than 3,700 rehabilitation organizations in the United States, Canada, and Sweden. CARF develops and maintains practical and relevant standards of quality for a range programs including TCs. Affiliation with regional, national and international TC associations, teaching hospitals and universities is another trend which clearly demonstrates the perceived importance of setting professional standards for program content, therapeutic approach, and staffing.

Prominent TC organizations include The Association of Therapeutic Communities, Therapeutic Communities of America, The European Federation of Therapeutic Communities and The Center for Therapeutic Community Research. In conjunction with a number of TCs worldwide, these organizations have been instrumental in helping to develop meaningful tools to help define "success rates" and measure outcomes at TCs.

The attempt to determine what constitutes 'success' in the TC model is a challenging task. Success is described by one expert as follows: "In the eyes of the therapeutic community staff, the successful therapeutic community graduate may be someone who takes no drugs, has no further convictions, and leads a busy and orderly life".

To date, there are not many independent longitudinal follow-up studies of TC "graduates." One particularly important source of information can be found in the Drug Abuse Treatment Outcomes Studies (DATOS) initiated in 1990 by the US National Institute on Drug Abuse (NIDA).There are a number of important conclusions reached by the DATOS research that are echoed both in studies carried out by individual TCs, as well as information gathered. One of the most significant findings is that retention predicts outcome. What this means is that the longer a resident remains in the TC program, the more likely they are to achieve the program goals and avoid returning to previous patterns and behaviours. This finding is important for the obvious reason that it underscores the link between good program planning and "successful" outcomes. Another important finding is that retention rates are linked to the integral role played by well trained professional staff in guiding residents through the therapeutic process.

In both cases, poor program planning and staffing decisions clearly result in higher rates of resident drop-out. Although DATOS provide important insights about current US trends and outcomes in relation to TCs, questions remain about the transferability of findings to a Canadian context. The common focus on post-treatment outcome in TC research can be understood in light of the fact that reductions in drug use and reconviction often reflect the real concern of funding agencies and public interest.

At the same time, a number of "pre-testing" methods have developed that are designed to help ensure that good decisions are made in setting up new TCs. Examples of these tools include a scale of essential TC elements, client matching protocols, and a treatment environmental risk index.

Operational Issues

When considering ways to ensure a well functioning TC, a number of operational issues arise. Factors to be considered include (1) optimal governance and management structures, (2) adequacy and reliability of on-going operational funding, (3) intake and referral systems, (4) transition planning for residents who complete the program.

In most TCs, funding is drawn from a range of sources including public and private organizations. The exception is San Francisco's Delancey Street which accepts no government funding. Regardless of the structure of operation and governance, a strong message that emerged from the research is the importance of drawing on experienced leadership in governance and management structures.

Paid professionals with first hand experience in human service delivery generally, but also the specific challenges presented by the TC model in particular, were identified by most TC operators as instrumental in defining key objectives, maintaining organizational and financial stability, and achieving high resident retention rates in TCs.

Another common element of governance and management found at many TCs is on-going consultation with social service providers, educational institutions, and vocational training institutes. In addition, some TCs have formal advisory boards made up of neighbours and service providers.

The formulation of a long-term funding strategy indicating how construction, operation and maintenance will be funded on an on-going basis is a common staple of most TCs. This type of funding strategy is particularly critical during phase-in and expansion stages when operational funding needs will necessarily be in transition. Another important planning tool for non-profit TCs are yearly audited financial statements which non-profit.TCs are required by law to produce. The benefit of yearly financial statements is that they provide the opportunity to track success in achieving the goals set in long-term strategies, as well as demonstrate good financial management.

The screening and intake process for TC residents is normally very rigorous and thorough. The intake process can include an initial visit or phone call, admission to a waiting list, an orientation process, one or more intake interviews, medical, legal and psychological assessments, and consent to treatment. The number of common intake and referral characteristics shared by the programs listed above is indicative of the commonalties across TCs generally.

The most important message to be taken from this important aspect of TC operations is that the intake and referral process should be carefully matched with the defined program goals and the needs of the chosen resident group. Another important element that should be noted is the relatively high proportion of residents who are referred through the criminal justice system. In this capacity, questions arise as to how critical this corrections-based referral system is to the overall success of TCs.

In the Canadian context, such referrals may or may not be expected or allowed, underscoring the importance of carefully considering linkages to a range of referral systems. A related issue for consideration is the decision about whether or not the TC will be local-serving only or open to referrals from a wider geographical area. If the decision is to accept referrals from a wide geographical area, impacts on the City of Vancouver must be considered, particularly in relation to risks associated with high drop-out rates.

Another critical aspect of TC operations corresponds with the final phases of treatment when residents are being prepared to leave the facility. Unless there are extenuating circumstances, most TCs aim to ensure that no resident leaves the program without a full-time job, a place to live and a support network. A host of challenges were identified by operators and experts in the field regarding the nature and extent of aftercare services.

First, because many programs are becoming shorter in duration (mainly due to funding challenges), the need for adequate aftercare has been escalating in recent years, in some cases dramatically. This increase has added to already existing challenges to meet the aftercare needs of residents in this critical phase of treatment.

Second, among the most pressing needs in aftercare services is transitional and supported housing that is safe and affordable, a social need that has proven a challenge in many cities and rural areas alike across Canada and the US.

Lastly, as indicated in the programmatic section of the report, an important aspect of good governance and operations is follow up research designed to ensure the continued success of TC 'graduates' after they leave the program. However, many TCs have indicated that they lack the funds to undertake meaningful longitudinal research that would enable TCs to track the success of their graduates, thereby identifying best practices, as well as program areas in need of improvement.

Locational Issues

Therapeutic Communities operate in a wide variety of settings including residential, industrial, mixed residential / commercial, and rural sites. TC facilities consist of purpose-built structures, as well as a range of converted buildings such as tenement housing, hotels, schools, churches or nursing homes. As highly structured, self-contained programs, TCs are designed to enhance the clients' experience of community within the residence, while at the same time seeking to minimize the facility's impact on the surrounding community.

However, in determining the feasibility and appropriateness of any new TC facility, a number of locational issues must be considered carefully. The mitigation of many negative neighbourhood impacts may be attributable to a number of factors. First, the self-contained nature of the TC means that most interaction with the surrounding neighbourhood is generally planned and controlled. Second, although TCs are not locked facilities, strict limits are placed on residents' comings and goings so the possibility of undesirable street activity associated with TC residents is reduced. Third, by establishing themselves in areas where pre-existing shifts in land use have taken place, TCs minimize the possibility of incompatible uses that can result in conflict.

Educational training provided by a TC typically consists of the goal of obtaining a General Equivalency Diploma (GED), some post-secondary coursework, and in exceptional cases, a university degree. Vocational skills training can include culinary arts, carpentry, general maintenance, mechanical systems, general contracting, computer skills, or substance abuse counselling. Other common supports provided at the TC include legal services, advocacy, and life skills counselling.

In the case of most TCs, because the majority of educational and therapeutic training is delivered on site, there appears to be little disruption on surrounding streets, and generally low impacts on traffic, noise and parking. However, the greater the number of partnerships with educational institutions, vocational training organizations or job placement sites that are not centralized in the TC, the greater the potential for neighbourhood disruption depending on the nature of the surrounding area.

Correspondingly, if a proposed TC chose to adopt the unusual entrepreneurial focus of the Delancey Street model, where fully operational businesses are located in or near the TC, increases in traffic, noise, parking, and general impacts on the nature of the neighbourhood, might be felt depending on the type of activity already located in the surrounding area.

Most TCs provide some level of primary health and dental care either on or off site. As a requirement for admission, many TCs insist that residents must be healthy enough to undertake physical labour and participate in therapeutic aspects of treatment. However, the reality is that most residents arrive with a number of underlying health issues relating to their past experiences with addiction, homelessness, or incarceration.Common health conditions include diabetes, hepatitis, HIV and asthma. A range of.opinions exist on the costs and benefits of providing a full spectrum of health care services on site.

The primary advantage to on-site health service is twofold. First, on-site health care reduces possible disruptions to the neighbourhood in the form of increased traffic to and from the site. And second, on-site care reduces the exposure of residents to negative external influences that might lead to relapse or failure to complete the program.

3

Counselling and Therapeutic Practices

The counselling experienced as healing by clients has at its core a vibrantly warm and honest relationship where the client feels held in the safety of the good heart space of the counsellor. The counsellor is experienced as providing an intense beingness for the client that embraces the client's suffering and provides solid ground created out of the crucible of the counsellor's own encounter with his or her shadow. The counsellor is emptied out of his/her own agenda and provides space for the client's experience. The counsellor can evoke the higher resources of the client.

The counselling is experienced as renewing and reconnecting the clients to his/her sense of self, of other and the lifeworld. The counselling relationship experienced as harming is described as being drained of human presence and transforming power. There is no alive human connection. The counsellor is experienced as insubstantial, and has no ability to hold traumatic experience. The counsellor's cold reception to the client's vulnerabilities has the power to shatter, fragment and splinter the client.

The counsellor is full of self. This fullness may be ego that manifests as dry intellectualising or playing manipulative games as a substitute for human presence. This may lead the client to terror, sickness and anxiety. The counsellor may be full of their own fears and are experienced by the client as chaotic, avoidant and overwhelmed. Their unavailability leads clients to experience emotional depletion, exhaustion and frustration.

The counsellor's self-righteousness, judgement and critical disengagement are experienced by clients as being belittled, condemned and diminished. The therapeutic encounter results in a weakening of the human potential for recovery. Both client and counsellor emerge as lesser human beings, with weakened relationships to self, others and the world.

Rennie uses grounded theory methodology to analyse dialogues of client experience. Ethnographers such as Kuehl, Newfield and Joanning (1990), O'Connor, Meakes and Pickering (1997), Sells, Smith and Moon (1996) and Smith, Yoshioka and Winton (1993) all use open format questions. Kuehl et al. (1990), Sells et al. (1996) and Smith et al. (1993) incorporate a form of content or discourse analysis to identify emergent themes and categories among the words people use to describe their counselling experiences. The majority of research completed on client experience has used one of the aforementioned paradigms.

Phenomenological approaches have been few and this is regretful given that phenomenology is particularly appropriate in explicating the depth and meaning of client experience. Phenomenology is an exploration of the essence of lived experience which Van Manen states, "is the study of the life-world as we immediately experience it pre-reflectively rather than as we conceptualise, categorise and reflect on it". Phenomenology has the potential to reveal client experience in its rich immediacy and vibrancy. Drier and Giorgi go further to state that the content of the phenomenological method is the data of experience, its meaning for the subject, and most importantly the essence of the experience. This approach views clients as experts in their own experiences, and the meanings they place upon those experiences.

Moustakas notes that the applicability of the phenomenological method to such research is evident by "the wholeness of the approach which aims at examining entities from many sides, angles, and perspectives until a unified vision of essences of a phenomenon or experience is achieved".

Philophonetics was developed by Yehuda Tagar and is an innovative contemporary Australian modality of psychotherapy. There was no a priori selection around modality. Ascribing to the phenomenological method applied by Giorgi and Schweitzer, the meaning structures of the client's experience were explicated. The explication process involves six separate identifiable stages, moving from idiographic to nomothetic.

Stage 1. Intuitive/holistic understanding of the raw data The first stage involved reading the transcribed interviews repeatedly if necessary, to achieve a holistic and intuitive understanding of the meanings attributed to the phenomena. From the outset of the research process, all preconceptions and judgements were bracketed.

Stage 2. Forming a constituent profile This stage involved the construction of a constituent profile, which summarises the raw data from each participant. A set of natural meaning units, or NMUs, are extracted. NMUs are self-definable, discrete segments of expression of individual aspects of the participant's experience. The purpose expressed in each of the extracted NMUs is reduced to central themes. Central themes express the meaning concisely, whilst maintaining the original mode of expression. Central themes reduce the NMUs to recognisable sentences conveying a discrete expression of experience. Finally, central themes that are repeated are distilled to a single theme. Central themes are then re-ordered to provide greater coherence of the data. The subsequent reconstituted list of central themes provides a non-repetitive list of descriptive meaning statements for each participant, which is termed the constituent profile.

Stage 3. Forming a thematic index: Constituent profiles of each participant are used as a basis to construct a 'thematic index', which highlights major themes that have emerged. The 'thematic index' enables the data to be moved from an idiographic level to a nomothetic level. Additionally, the 'thematic index' establishes a referent system that allows any emergent themes to be easily accessed. The delineated meaning units of each constituent profile are combined and re-ordered into one list of emergent themes. Constituent profiles are searched for referents that are extracted and listed separately. Referents are specific words that highlight the meaning of the experience being researched. The thematic index establishes a non-repetitive, sequenced list of meaning statements and referents used to search for interpretative themes. The thematic index contains the constituent profile statements attributed to singular meanings of experience. In each case the referent that emphasises the meaning being portrayed is identified as a key for any subsequent searches. From this point on the data is examined collectively.

Stage 4. Searching the thematic index: This enables the comparison of referents, central themes and constituent profile to form a set of interpretative themes. Interpretative themes are statements that succinctly capture the meanings portrayed through the constituent profiles, and do not necessarily retain the original mode of expression. Using the referents as a key, the constituent profiles and central themes are searched to explicate interpretative themes, which enable the formation of the extended description. The 'search' command, within word processing software, was used to find referents in sentences within the central themes and constituent profile. The sentences matching the referents are grouped under the relevant referents. The grouped referents and sentences are then individually explored and assigned to a developed interpretative theme. During the overlap search interpretative themes that have been identified are also examined for their relationship to each other within the context which they have been used in the constituent profiles and central themes.

Stage 5. Arriving at a extended description Interpretative themes are used to rigorously explicate meaning attributed to the phenomena under investigation.

Stage 6. Synthesis of extended description This is a summary of the interpretative themes to produce an in-depth picture of clients' experience of the counselling process.

The themes of psychotherapy reported as being healing will be clustered under the following embracing interpretative themes:

1. Clients desire the counsellor to facilitate with safety the opening up of deep layers of the clients' experience

2. Clients desire to experience an honest and authentic encounter with the counsellor
3. Clients require focus of session to be on their agenda so that they feel empowered and fully respected by the counsellor
4. Clients need to experience the therapeutic encounter as contributing to their ongoing personal development.

The four corresponding interpretative themes of psychotherapy experienced as harming are:

1. Clients experience counsellor as abandoning them in threatening experiences
2. Clients experience counsellor as acting inauthentically.
3. Clients feel that they are "hijacked" by the counsellor's personal agenda
4. Clients experience the therapeutic encounter as undermining their esteem and weakening their coping skills.

Clients desire the counsellor to facilitate with safety the opening up of deep layers of the client's experience This interpretative theme includes the cluster of themes of providing a supportive, comfortable atmosphere, and experiencing an accepting counsellor who makes them feel valued. It includes experiencing a relationship with a counsellor who is fully present and thus experiencing being seen, heard and fully understood by the counsellor.

It involves experiencing the counsellor as promoting a self affirming relationship with one's self and one's experience. Clients feel safe when they can expose the deep layers of their suffering and feel held by the counsellor. In the space of the client exposing deep layers of pain, clients want to experience the space as a completely sealed place free from intrusions. The space is created and sustained by the counsellor through complete attention and focus on the client. It is a place without leaky windows or holes in the walls, an inner room sustained by the counsellor and totally consecrated to providing an accepting and undisturbed focus for the client's deepest pain. For clients there is the quality of an "impenetrable space" where one can expose ones most vulnerable self without the demands and pressures of daily "normal" life.

Clients also describe this space as a "heart space" and the space of intimate profoundly concentrated listening on behalf of the counsellor. Clients describe the strong solid reliable experience of a counsellor as the counsellor not being overwhelmed by the clients deep feelings and traumas. The counsellor holds the space in a calm and peaceful way and provides focused listening. Tina captures the essence of the experience of this connection between the safe space and deep inner issues:

Clients desire to experience an honest authentic encounter with the counsellor The following cluster of themes are recurrent in the clients' interviews. Firstly, the therapist being experienced for who they really are and not hiding behind qualifications or artificial intellectual power. Secondly, the therapist not acting or playing games with the client. Thirdly, the therapist having insight into his/her own limitations and own baggage, and maintaining confidentiality. Finally, the therapist not using subtle emotional, sexual, mental or spiritual suggestions in a manipulative way to seduce clients.

Clients speak about wanting to relate to a real person not a "phoney". The experience of realness comes from sensing that the counsellor is also human, understands pain, knows human frailties but in the counselling session can combine that quality of knowing pain and human frailties with stability, centredness and inspiration.

Authenticity in the counsellor is the experience of the person being energetically present to the relationship with the client. Clients describe authenticity as the experience of the counsellor acknowledging his/her essential humanity and the client's "essence" or who they are as an unique human being. The quality of authenticity includes the experience for clients of expecting confidentiality in the sense of sharing their experiences with a person who is holding them respectfully. It is about trusting the counsellor to uphold the safety and secretness of the clients' revelations.

At the heart of the gesture of honouring authentically the counselling contract is the client experiencing respect from the counsellor. It's about not gossiping to others or to themselves about the clients' frailties or experiences. This is the gesture of the counsellor being present to their own knowledge but without the drive of ego to demonstrate what he/she knows. It is a dance of givingness choreographed by the client's needs. It is the wisdom of apprehending what will strengthen the client combined with the humility of accepting that all of one's counselling skills are only relevant in so far as they support the client's relationship with his/her experiences.

Clients want the focus of the relationship to be on their agenda so that they feel empowered and fully respected by the counsellor. The clients experience of directing the pace of the counselling session, of not being pushed by the counsellor, of their own agenda not the counsellors running the session are encompassed by this interpretative theme. The experience of being held by the counsellor by the client is one which the counsellor builds on something emerging from the client and is the nature of a "joining".

The counsellor comes to "to meet" the client without any of his/her own baggage. It is a clear space where the client experiences the counsellor as seeing the client without preconceived worldviews. The counsellor's response brings about flourishing and healing in the clients' experiences because it ex experienced as nurturing.

Clients want the counsellor's personal life to be contained "to be put on the backburner" so the counsellor can be fully present to create a meeting with the client that transcends the counsellor's own limited ego. The counsellor intimately dances with the client's inner life and needs, always in response to the needs of the client. When that is absent then the dance of relationship is lost and the counsellor is experienced as disconnected from the client, alone, running their own "content agenda".

Clients need to experience the therapeutic encounter as relieving their presenting distress and contributing to their ongoing personal development. The cluster of themes includes experiencing the counsellor as promoting a self affirming relationship with ones experience, experiencing carthersis or down loading of deep emotions, experiencing the counsellor as providing skills for ongoing use, and experiencing the counselling processes providing benefits beyond the therapeutic relationship.

That quality of safe holding by the counsellor of the client's experience facilitates the carthartic experience. This carthartic experience has the aspect of uncovering, bringing into the light of knowledge, that which was previously unseen or unknown and the release of dead emotional weight which was burdening the client. Clients refer to this dimension of the carthartic experience as "lifting the weight of the world off their shoulders". It is the process of "unloading excess baggage". This is experienced as reduction in size of the problem.

Clients experience a self affirming relationship when what they conceived of as failure, or suffering in their life, is transformed through the counselling process to produce new insight and awareness into their potential strength. This transformative process empowers clients and profoundly releases their inner life so they no longer experience being blocked or "stuck". Clients also want to develop strategies and feel inner changes to cope with their problem.

As a culmination of the counselling experience clients want personal change and growth in themselves and their lives. They want increased capacity to deal with their relationship to self, experience, to others and to their relationship to the life-world. Clients want greater insight and abilities to act effectively. Counselling results in personal development when the client experiences support to explore the depths of his/her experiences. Clients value support and effective tools for moving through the trauma and confusion to a place of perspective and clarity.

Clients experience of a threatening counselling situation is one in which they are "overwhelmed by the pain with no support". Overexposure to inner trauma without being given adequate skills or supports by the counsellor is a frequent complaint of the clients who felt harmed by the counsellor. Rhonda describes the terror that led to a nervous breakdown:

Clients experience counsellor as acting inauthentically Clients describe their longing for acknowledgment of their feelings not "some phoney, glib intellectual response" or "smart games". Clients feel that they are hijacked by the counsellor's personal agenda. There were three aspects to being pushed. The first was the clients' sense of the counsellor failing to facilitate the clients' experience of empowerment or control over their problem.

Clients also want to take responsibility for their own pacing in the session. They are critical of counsellors who pushed them in relation to time and pace. Those counsellors who force them to open up too much too quickly, and those counsellors who terminate sessions too quickly when too much was still open and unresolved are experienced as harmful by clients. Clients describe the experience as "damaging" their bodies and their hearts, overexposing, shocking, painful and disorienting. The worst experiences clients describe as "terrifying".

Clients describing this terror, experience it in the body as a panic attack, or as an energetic collapse so that simple tasks like driving a vehicle are impossible. Clients experience the therapeutic encounter as undermining their esteem and weakening their coping skills. Clients mention that feeling judged by the counsellor interfers with their capacity to deal productively with their problems. Judgement was associated with three experiences in relationship to the counsellor. The first was feeling devalued in the sense of feeling dismissed, as though they were unimportant and irrelevant to the counsellor.

The counselling experience most valued by clients is a vibrantly warm and honest relationship where the client feels held in the safety of the good heart space of the counsellor. The counsellor provides an intense beingness and companionship for the client that embraces his/her suffering and provides solid ground on which to stand among the emotional maelstrom. This substantial ground is created out of the crucible of the counsellor's own life where he/she has encountered shadows and light and can face without fear or judgement the human demons.

The counsellor has transformed these encounters into wisdom. The counsellor is emptied of his/her own agenda and provides a crucible for the client's experience. The counsellor has the feeling space to be fully present to the client and can fully join the client's experience to understand it from the inside. The counsellor is part of the dance of givingness that is choreographed by the client's needs. The counsellor's words and actions are gifts to the client, jewels of new meaning.

The counsellor can evoke the higher resources of the client, call forth the strength and new power from the client and plant seeds of new awareness. Out of this I-thou encounter with the counsellor, a third force arises, greater than either person. This force births that which is highest in the client, and it is the midwife of healing. Its child is wisdom. It is a renewal and reconnection to the client's sense of self, of other and the life-world in a way that promises more insightful, richer and flourishing experiences.

Harmful Counselling and Psychotherapy

A harmful counselling relationship is drained of human presence and transforming power. There is no alive human connection, no two way glow. The counsellor is experienced as insubstantial, with no solidity, no ability to hold traumatic experience or pain. The client meets a cold reception from exposing himself/herself to the counsellor that has the power to shatter, fragment and splinter the client. The counsellor is full of self-concerns and has no space for the client. This fullness may be ego that manifests as dry intellectualising or playing manipulative games as a substitute for human presence in the counsellor. In the client this may lead to terror, and physical symptoms of sickness and anxiety.

The counsellor may be full of their own fears and are experienced by the client as unbalanced, chaotic, avoidant and overwhelmed. Both states in counsellors' unavailability to clients results in clients experiencing emotional depletion, exhaustion and frustration. The counsellor's self-righteousness, judgement and critical disengagement from the clients problems, are experienced by clients as being belittled, condemned and diminished. There is a weak human connection and the therapeutic encounter results in a weakening of the human potential for recovery. Both client and counsellor emerge as lesser human beings, with weakened relationships to self, others and the world.

Preventing Suicide

According to WHO estimates approximately one million people are likely to commit suicide in the year 2000. Suicide is among the top 10 causes of death in every country, and one of the three leading causes of death in the 15 to 35-year age group. The psychological and social impact of suicide on the family and society is immeasurable. On average, single suicide intimately affects at least six other people. If a suicide occurs in a school or workplace it has an impact on hundreds of people.

The burden of suicide can be estimated in terms of DALYs (disability-adjusted life years). According to this indicator, in 1998 suicide was responsible for 1.8% of the total burden of disease worldwide, varying between 2.3% in high-income countries and 1.7% in low-income countries. This is equal to the burden due to wars and homicide, roughly twice the burden of diabetes, and equal to the burden of birth asphyxia and trauma.

Suicide is now understood as a multidimensional disorder, which results from a complex interaction of biological, genetic, psychological, sociological and environmental factors. Research has shown that between 40% and 60% of people who commit suicide had seen a physician in the month prior to suicide; of these, many more had seen a general physician rather than a psychiatrist. In countries where the mental health services are not well developed, the proportion of people in suicidal crisis consulting a general physician is likely to be higher. To identify, assess and manage suicidal patients is an important task of the physician, who has a crucial role in suicide prevention.

Studies from both developing and developed countries reveal an overall prevalence of mental disorders of 80-100% in cases of completed suicide. It is estimated that the lifetime risk of suicide in people with mood disorders is 6-15%; with alcoholism, 7-15%; and with schizophrenia, 4-10%. Suicide is in itself not a disease, nor necessarily the manifestation of a disease, but mental disorders are a major factor associated with suicide.

However, a substantial proportion of people who commit suicide die without having seen a mental health professional. Hence improved detection, referral and management of psychiatric disorders in primary care is an important step in suicide prevention. A common finding in those who commit suicide is the presence of more than one disorder. The common disorders occurring together are alcoholism and mood disorder (i.e. depression), and personality disorder and other psychiatric disorders.

All types of mood disorders have been associated with suicide. These include bipolar affective disorder, depressive episode, recurrent depressive disorder and persistent mood disorders (e.g. cyclothymia and dysthymia), which form categories F31-F34 in ICD-10 (1). Suicide is therefore a significant risk in unrecognized and untreated depression. Depression has a high prevalence in the general population and is not recognized by many as a disease. It is estimated that 30% of patients seen by a physician are suffering from depression. Roughly 60% of those who do seek treatment initially contact a general practitioner. It is a special challenge for the physician to work with both physical disease and psychological disorders simultaneously.

In many instances, depression is masked and patients present only with somatic complaints. Common presenting symptoms of depression are:

— Tiredness

— Sadness

— Lack of concentration

— Anxiety

— Irritability

— Sleep disturbances

— Pain in different parts of the body.

These symptoms should alert the physician to the presence of depression and lead to an assessment of the suicide risk. Specific clinical features associated with increased risk of suicide in depression are:

— Persistent insomnia

— Self-neglect

— Severe illness (particularly psychotic depression)

Collaborating with the psychiatrist and ensuring that adequate and appropriate treatment is given is a crucial function of the physician. In typical depressive episodes, the individual usually suffers from:

— depressed mood (sadness)

— loss of interest and enjoyment

— reduced energy (fatiguability and diminished activity)

— Impaired memory

— Agitation

— Panic attacks.

The following factors increase the risk of suicide in people with depression:

— Age below 25 years in men

— Early phase of the illness

— Abuse of alcohol

— Depressed phase of a bipolar disorder

— Mixed (manic-depressive) state

— Psychotic mania.

Depression is an important factor in suicide among both adolescents and the elderly but those with late onset of depression are at a higher risk. Recent advances in the treatment of depression are very relevant for suicide prevention in primary care. Education of the general practitioner in identifying and treating depression was found to reduce suicide in Sweden. Patients on regular lithium maintenance therapy have been found to have lower suicide risk.

Alcoholism (both alcohol abuse and dependence on alcohol) is a frequent diagnosis in those who have committed suicide, particularly in young people. There are biological, psychological and social explanations for the correlation between suicide and alcoholism. Specific factors associated with increased suicide risk among alcoholics are:

— Early onset of alcoholism

— Long history of drinking

— High level of dependence

— Depressed mood

— Poor physical health

— Poor work performance

— Family history of alcoholism

— Recent disruption or loss of a major interpersonal relationship.

Suicide is the largest single cause of premature death among schizophrenics. Specific risk factors for suicide are:

— Young unemployed male

— Recurrent relapses

— Fear of deterioration, especially in those of high intellectual ability

— Positive symptoms of suspiciousness and delusions

— Depressive symptoms.

Recent studies on young people who committed suicide have shown a high prevalence (20-50%) of personality disorder. The personality disorders that are more frequently associated with suicide are borderline personality and antisocial personality disorders. Histrionic and narcissistic personality disorders and certain psychological traits such as impulsivity and aggression, have also been associated with suicide.

Among anxiety disorders, panic disorder has been most frequently associated with suicide, followed by obsessive-compulsive disorder (OCD). Somatoform disorder and eating disorders (anorexia nervosa and bulimia) are also related to suicidal behaviour.

Suicide risk is increased in chronic physical illness. In addition, there is generally an increased rate of psychiatric disorder, especially depression, in people with physical illness. Chronicity, disability and negative prognosis are correlated with suicide.

Epilepsy has been associated with increased suicide. The increase has been attributed to the increased impulsivity, aggressivity and chronic disability associated with epilepsy. Spinal and brain injuries also increase the risk of suicide. Recent studies have shown that after a stroke - particularly in the presence of posterior lesions, which cause greater disability and physical impairment - 19% of patients are depressed and suicidal.

The risk of suicide is highest at the time of diagnosis and in the first two years of the terminal illness with an increase in risk in cases of progressive malignancy. Pain is a significant contributing factor to suicide.

HIV infection and AIDS represent an increased risk of suicide in the young, with high suicide rates. The risk is greater at the time of confirmation of the diagnosis and in the early stages of the illness. Intravenous drug users are at still higher risk.

Other chronic medical conditions such as chronic renal disease, liver disease, bone and joint disorders, cardiovascular disease and gastrointestinal disorders are implicated in suicide. Disabilities of locomotion, blindness and deafness can also precipitate a suicide. In recent years euthanasia and assisted suicide have become issues that may confront the physician. Active euthanasia is illegal in almost all jurisdictions, and assisted suicide is enmeshed in moral, ethical and philosophical controversy.

In the majority of countries, more males commit suicide than females; the male/female ratio varies from country to country. China is the only country in which female suicides outnumber male suicides in rural areas and are approximately equal to male suicides in urban areas. The elderly and the younger age groups are at increased risk of suicide. Recent data suggest an increase in suicide rates in middle-aged men.

Divorced, widowed and single people are at increased risk of suicide. Marriage appears to be protective for males in terms of suicide risk but not significantly so for females. Certain occupational groups such as veterinary surgeons, pharmacists, dentists, farmers and medical practitioners have a higher risk of suicide. There is no obvious explanation for this finding, though access to lethal means, work pressure, social isolation and financial difficulties might be the reasons.

There are fairly strong associations between unemployment rates and suicide rates, but the nature of these associations is complex. The effects of unemployment are probably mediated by factors such as poverty, social deprivation, domestic difficulties and hopelessness. On the other hand, people with mental disorders are more likely to be unemployed than people in good mental health. At any rate, due consideration should be given to the difference in the significance of recent loss of employment and long-term unemployment: greater risk is associated with the former.

In some countries suicides are more frequent in urban areas, whereas in others they occur more frequently in rural areas. Migration - with its attendant problems of poverty, poor housing, lack of social support and unmet expectations - increases the risk of suicide. Certain social factors, such as the ready availability of the means of committing suicide and stressful life events play a significant role in increasing the risk of suicide. A number of clinically useful individual and sociodemographic factors are associated with suicide. They include:

— Psychiatric disorders (generally depression, alcoholism and personality disorders);

— Physical illness (terminal, painful or debilitating illness, AIDS);

— Previous suicide attempts;

— Family history of suicide, alcoholism and/or other psychiatric disorders;

— Divorced, widowed or single status;

— Living alone (socially isolated);

— Unemployed or retired;

— Bereavement in childhood.

If the patient is under psychiatric treatment, the risk is higher in:

— Those who have recently been discharged from hospital;

— Those who have made previous suicide attempts.

In addition, recent life stressors associated with increased risk of suicide include:

— Marital separation;

— Bereavement:

— Family disturbances;

— Change in occupational or financial status;

— Rejection by a significant person;

— Shame and threat of being found guilty.

The physician may be confronted with a variety of conditions and situations associated with suicidal behaviour. An elderly male, recently widowed, treated for depression, living alone, with a history of attempted suicide, and a young lady with a few scratches on the forearm whose boyfriend has left her are two contrasting examples. In reality, most patients fall between those two extremes and they may fluctuate from one category to the other. When physicians have a reasonable indication that the patient could be suicidal, they face the dilemma of how to proceed. Some physicians are uncomfortable with suicidal patients.

If the physician decides to proceed, the first and most immediate step is mentally to allocate adequate time to the patient, even though many others may be waiting outside the room. By showing a willingness to understand, the physician starts to establish a positive rapport with the patient. It is not easy to ask patients about their suicidal ideas. It is helpful to lead into the topic gradually. A sequence of useful questions is:

1. Do you feel unhappy and helpless?
2. Do you feel desperate?
3. Do you feel unable to face each day?
4. Do you feel life is a burden?
5. Do you feel life is not worth living?
6. Do you feel like committing suicide?

If a patient is emotionally disturbed, with vague suicidal thoughts, the opportunity of ventilating thoughts and feelings to a physician who shows concern may be sufficient. Nevertheless, an opportunity for further follow-up should be left open, particularly if the patient has inadequate social support. Whatever the problem, the feelings of the suicidal person are usually a triad of helplessness, hopelessness and despair. The three most common states are:

1. *Ambivalence*: The majority of suicidal patients are ambivalent till the very end. There is a see-saw battle between the wish to live and the wish to die. If the ambivalence is used by the physician to increase the wish to live, the suicide risk may be reduced.
2. *Impulsivity*: Suicide is an impulsive phenomenon and impulse by its very nature is transient. If support is provided at the moment of impulse, the crisis may be defused.
3. *Rigidity* Suicidal people are constricted in their thinking, mood and action and their reasoning is dichotomized in terms of either/or. By exploring

several possible alternatives to death with the suicidal patient, the physician gently makes the patient realize that there are other options, even if they are not ideal.

The physician should assess the available support systems, identify a relative, friend, acquaintance or other person who would be supportive to the patient, and solicit that person's help. Entering into a "no suicide" contract is a useful technique in suicide prevention. Other people close to the patient can be included in negotiating the contract. The negotiation of thecontract can promote discussion of various relevant issues. In the majority of instances patients respect the promises they give to a physician. Contracting is appropriate only when patients have control over their actions.

In the absence of severe psychiatric disorder or suicidal intent, the physician can initiate and arrange pharmacological treatment, generally with antidepressants, and psychological (cognitive behaviour) therapy. The majority of people benefit from continuing contacts; these should be structured to meet individual needs. Except for the treatment of underlying diseases, few persons require support for longer than two or three months and the focus of the support should be providing hope, encouraging independence, and helping the patient to learn different ways of coping with life stressors.

Patients should be referred to a psychiatrist when they have:

— A psychiatric disorder;

— A history of a previous suicide attempt;

— A family history of suicide, alcoholism and psychiatric disorder;

— Physical ill-health;

— No social support.

Psychiatric Services

Counselling is a type of Psychotherapy of the supportive and educative type. Biological or pharmacological treatments have achieved a sophisticated and highly organised state of development in Ireland over the last fifty years. The same could not be said for psychological therapy services. These are under-developed and poorly resourced in Ireland, unlike Europe, the US and United Kingdom.

The result is that psychiatric services lack the effectiveness, efficiency and balance that a comprehensive holistic approach brings. "Biological priority; psychological superiority" is an aphorism or ideal for mature mental health services. Although expertise and urgency are prioritised in the physical and pharmacological treatment of mental disorder, mental health professionals are required to develop superior skills and expertise in the psychological therapies compared to their colleagues in other health care disciplines.

There is a growing evidence base underpinning the use of psychotherapy in the management of a wide variety of conditions including psychoses, eating disorders and severe personality disorders. For some disorders, psychological treatments are the treatment of choice for example; whilst in others they are an adjunct to medication.

Modern psychiatry and psychotherapy service emphasises the effectiveness of a hub and spoke model, involving experts providing treatment and disseminating knowledge by training, supervision and consultation with others throughout the Mental Health System.

Psychological therapies make up one of the two main classes of treatment for mental health problems (the other being physical treatments). Over the last 50 years there have been major advances in psychotherapeutic treatments and today various forms of psychological therapies are widely practised within the Health Service, in the voluntary sector and in private practice. Public demand for psychologically informed treatments has also risen - partly due to increasing public dissatisfaction with medication only as a treatment for emotional disorders and partly due to the general trend of people becoming more open to the idea of working through their symptoms with a suitably trained professional in a therapeutic environment.

There is also demand for the therapies from those front line professionals responsible for managing services. Demand for all forms of psychotherapy outstrips supply. Today a wide range of mental health problems, including those with severe and enduring mental illness can be appropriately treated by one or more of the many forms of psychological treatments. In general, treatments may be offered for relatively short periods or be open-ended. They may be offered to individuals, families or to groups. With some adaptations they can be provided for children and adolescents.

The format of treatment can also differ in terms of intensity (e.g. five times a week or once a week or once a month), the setting (in-patient or community based) and the extent to which non-psychosocial treatments (such as medication) are offered adjunctively. Psychotherapy and

Psychological Therapies are synonyms and used interchangeably. In counselling there is generally less emphasis on theory than on practice, and self awareness of a general sort is emphasised more than personal therapy.

Strupp's well known definition describes psychotherapy as "an interpersonal process designed to modify feelings, cognitions, attitudes and behaviour which have proved troublesome to the person seeking help from a trained professional." A useful way to categorise psychotherapy according to theoretical basis and clinical technique is as follows:

— *Transference Therapies* namely psychoanalysis and psychoanalytic / psychodynamic psychotherapy. These are longer-term processes (can be a year or more) and allow unconscious conflicts in the patient the opportunity to be re-enacted and interpreted in the relationship with the therapist.

— *Cognitive and Behavioural Therapies* are structured treatment approaches derived from cognitive and behavioural theories. Cognitive techniques (such as challenging negative automatic thoughts) and behavioural techniques (such as activity scheduling and behavioural experiments) are used with the main aim of relieving symptoms by changing maladaptive thoughts and beliefs.

— *Group and Systemic Therapies* focus on the relational context and address patterns of interaction and meaning and aim to facilitate personal and interpersonal resources within a system as a whole.

Each approach or category has differences in the way in which the relationship between counsellor/therapist and client/patient is conducted. Counselling, unlike the psychotherapies, tends to be conducted without any exploration of the relationship between the patient and the therapist. In psychotherapy the therapeutic relationship is often a central focus and a route to the exploration of past and present relationships and personal difficulties in the patient.

In the training of transference and group psychotherapists, extensive theoretical learning and formal personal therapy are essential requirements. These trainings are demanding and time consuming and need to be nurtured and supported within the professions to realise their maximum benefits to the overall quality of health care provision. Roth and Fonaghy differentiate therapies primarily in terms of the following major classes:

— Psychodynamic Psychotherapy

— Behavioural and Cognitive Behavioural

— Interpersonal Therapy

— Strategic or Systematic Psychotherapy

— Supportive and Experiential Psychotherapy

— Group Psychotherapy

Within a Mental Health Service there are three types of Psychotherapy expertise and delivery based on Cawleys developmental framework:-

— *Type A* - Psychological treatment as an integral component of Mental Health Care. This refers to the psychotherapeutic skills required by all mental health and social care professionals.

— *Type B* - Eclectic Psychological Therapy and Counselling. This refers to the Psychotherapeutic skills needed by a broadly trained mental health/ social care professional (nurse, occupational therapist, social worker, clinical psychologist or psychiatrist) with a special interest in Psychotherapy who treats patients but does not act in a senior consultative or training capacity.

— *Type C* - Formal Psychotherapies. This refers to the specialist therapeutic skills required by a professional working for the majority of his/her time in the speciality i.e. Consultant Psychotherapist level with a significant responsibility for teaching and supervising others.

Cost of Psychotherapy

The cost of psychotherapy involves more than determining the price of treatment. The cost of psychological ill health to the individual, his/her friends and family and society is immeasurable. Mental ill health produces other social costs in terms of A&E department visits, GP appointments, medication, medical and psychiatric inpatient hospital admissions. The cost of psychotherapy, therefore, must not be calculated solely by the price of clinical sessions but by the impact of the treatment on reducing the human and social costs and the demand on other facilities within the health care system, for example, General Practice and the medical specialities.

Several studies provide evidence of the savings produced by psychotherapy. One study of patients with severe personality disorder suggested that inpatient psychoanalytic psychotherapy produced savings of £7,423 per patient in terms of reduced usage of health service resources. Gabbard reviewed the impact of psychotherapy on costs of care, from published studies between 1984-94 and concluded that psychotherapy led to a reduction in costs for most severe psychiatric conditions, particularly in relation to reduced inpatient costs and employment related savings. Five randomly assigned trials indicated that family therapy produced statistically significant cost savings in the treatment of schizophrenia.

Three recent trials at the Institute of Psychiatry in London have considered how the addition of psychotherapy to usual treatments can effect the use of health and community-care services. Those patients who received psychotherapy used hospital and community services less than the control groups.

In the setting up of a Psychotherapy Service according to the British Psychological Society and the Royal College of Psychiatrists the main recommendations were:

a) The Service should provide a comprehensive, co-ordinated and integrated assessment, treatment and consultation service in all the major psychological therapies using all existing resources to full effect.

b) The Service should ensure that a comprehensive range of psychological therapies is available to the population in need, wherever possible in accessible locations. In the community, primary care and community mental health practitioners will provide most psychological therapies with support, teaching and supervision from psychological therapy specialists. A specialist psychotherapy service is likely to require some centralisation.

c) Ideally there should be at least one specialist in each of the major psychological therapies provided e.g. transference therapies, cognitive and behavioural therapies and systemic and group therapies.

Roth and Fonaghy in "What Works for Whom?" describes the evidence based context for developing comprehensive treatment services for specific disorders. The emphasis is on providing a wide range of treatments including:

— Psychodynamic (Psychoanalytic) Psychotherapy

— Behavioural and Cognitive Psychotherapy

— Interpersonal Psychotherapy

— Strategic or Systemic Psychotherapies (Family)

— Supportive and Experiential Psychotherapies

— Group Therapies

Roth and Fonaghy's philosophy is that psychological treatments should be readily available to patients who would benefit from them, rather than in an ad-hoc and non-evidence based way. In Ireland to date, there has been little strategic planning of the psychotherapy services. Services including the National Counselling Service have been resourced in response to crisis situations instead of part of a long term evidence based strategy for development of psychotherapeutic services.

The Department of Health in England published *Evidence Based Clinical Practice Guidelines on Treatment Choice in Psychological Therapies and Counselling*. The guidelines include:

— Effectiveness of all types of therapy depends on the patient and the therapist forming a good working relationship.

— The patient's age, sex, social class or ethnic group should not determine access to therapy.

— In considering psychological therapies, more severe or complex mental health problems should receive secondary, specialist assessment.

— Therapies of fewer than eight sessions are unlikely to be optimally effective for most moderate to severe mental health problems.

— Counselling is not recommended as the main intervention for severe and complex mental health problems or personality disorders.

— A co-existing personality disorder may make treatment of most disorders more difficult and possibly less effective; indications of personality disorder include forensic history, severe relationship difficulties, and recurrent complex problems.

— Patient preference should inform treatment choice, particularly where the research evidence does not indicate a clear choice of therapy.

— The skill and experience of the therapist should also be taken into account. More complex problems, and those where patients are poorly motivated, require the more skilful therapist.

The Health Care Strategy 2001 identified four priority areas for the development of Mental Health Services; services for the elderly, child and adolescent services, eating disorder services and suicide prevention. Improving quality of care in all these areas requires increased resources in Psychotherapy.

The National Counselling Service of Ireland's Annual Report 2002 clearly outlines the need for Psychotherapy services. In their first report they state 'Between September 2000 and September 2001 almost 2000 adults who experienced abuse in childhood sought counselling from the National Counselling Service. Of these almost 700 identified that they were abused as children in Institutional settings'. In Ireland to date we have no accurate estimate of need in other settings.

Amnesty International Report of Mental Health: In Chapter 3, Amnesty International report that under Planning for the Future, Ireland is obliged to equitably secure the provision of a sufficient number of hospitals, clinics and other health facilities and the promotion and support of the establishment of institutions providing counselling and mental health services. In Chapter 5, they recommend that a comprehensive range of therapies, in addition to pharmacotherapy, is available to everyone with mental illness and cites an over reliance on medication.

Psychological therapy interventions in several major psychiatric diagnoses have been shown to cost no more than standard care (owing to reduced offset costs), while producing consistently better outcomes. The need for psychological therapies is emphasised by both professionals and consumers:

a) Psychiatrists feel they lack the time and adequate setting in which to practice their therapeutic skills with a consequent lowering of morale and difficulty in recruitment.

b) Users of psychiatric services consistently call for more 'talking treatments' and complain that psychiatrists rely excessively on physical methods of treatment.

c) A recent report on the state of in-patient psychiatric wards depicted an un-therapeutic environment in which staff felt beleaguered and patients dissatisfied and specifically called for more psychological treatments in inpatient settings.

d) Users and providers experience an unmet need for psychological therapies, and this is a crisis that affects mental health professionals. If nothing is done

> to tackle this problem there is a risk that an increasingly limited biological model will dominate policy-makers' view of psychiatry, pushing psychiatrists further towards a role of social control rather of therapeutic intervention.

Access to psychological therapy services in Ireland is limited. This is underlined by the number of Psychologists registered with the Psychological Society of Ireland. Clinical psychology services provide some of the range of psychological treatments often at both primary and secondary care levels. As a result invariably they have long waiting lists for assessment and treatment. In mental health services, Community Psychiatric Nurses, Social Workers and Occupational Therapists may have training in counselling or psychotherapy and could provide this service to a small number of patients on their caseload. However, these overloaded professionals have great difficulty in setting aside time to provide these treatments in the face of constant demands on them to provide acute care and crisis management.

There are no Consultant Psychotherapists in Ireland. According to the recommendations of The Royal College of Psychiatrists a minimum staffing level should be one WTE Consultant Psychotherapist per 200,000 of the population. A number of mental health professionals in Ireland currently have training in a variety of Psychotherapies. However the current lack of organisation of services is highly inefficient and does not permit these highly trained professionals to provide expert treatment to the patient population. This waste of a valuable resource is regrettable.

Within the voluntary sector, services in psychological therapy and counselling exist but access to these services, as with other services suffer from long waiting lists and limited resources. There is much to be gained from a partnership with well organised, statutory psychological services. The provision of psychological therapy services and training there are some agreed key elements:

— The development of psychological treatment services should build on existing resources wherever possible, rather than disrupting, dismantling or replacing established services in order to create an "ideal" model.

— Essential clinical components of a service are assessment, treatment and a consultative service to other treatment providers and potential referring agents.

— A service should be comprehensive. It should offer a range of treatments and provision should be made for the introduction of additional models of treatment.

— The clinical service should be integrated across all levels of health care and provide treatment at different levels of expertise.

— There should be collaboration between the various providers to ensure clear referral channels, comprehensive assessment and flexibility in treatment approach. Partnership with the voluntary sector is an important aspect of this collaboration.

— Services should be efficient and effective. The services should provide treatments, that meet assessed need and the treatments provided should be clinically effective.

— Services should be accessible to the whole community.

— All practitioners of psychological therapies should be proficient in the treatments they deliver. This has implications for training and three levels of training within each model of therapy are recommended.

— The preferred model arising out of the recent literature is a "consortium of psychological therapy providers". This means that a number of professional groupings with training in different types of the psychological therapies and at different levels of expertise would link together to offer a comprehensive psychological assessment and treatment service at different levels within the service.

A number of dimensions can be identified when considering the need for psychological therapy services. A comprehensive range of psychological therapies should be provided at primary, secondary and tertiary levels. The range of therapies should include Psychoanalytic/ Psychodynamic, Cognitive Behavioural, Group Analytic and Systemic Family Therapy.

Determined efforts to widen the availability of psychotherapy to those on low incomes, males with personality disorders and the seriously mentally ill must be in the forefront of any modern Psychological Therapy Service. There has in the past been pressure to restrict mental health service psychiatric treatments, including psychological therapies, to the 'seriously mentally ill', a term which sometimes excludes chronic psycho-neurotic disorders, severe personality disorders, and other disabling psychiatric disorders.

Restricting psychiatric treatments to patients with psychotic illness would exclude treatment for both highly dysfunctional but readily treatable psycho-neurotic disorders (e.g. panic disorder, agoraphobia), and for patients with complex personality and behavioural problems who make heavy demands on both GPs and mental health services. Where these restrictions have been introduced, they have not found favour with patients or their GPs.

Small therapeutic changes in patients with personality disorders may be critical in terms of improved life adjustment and expectancy, particularly for patients who make large and chaotic demands on primary care and mental health services. Effective treatment may require a prolonged psychotherapeutic input. Clinical evidence indicates that this is productive in terms of reduced behavioural disturbance and demand on services. Further research is required to establish a systematic evidence-base for psychological treatments of patients with personality disorders.

This will result in a range of psychological therapies being provided in a range of settings. Co-ordination is essential in order to ensure efficiency and accessibility of services and is required between practitioners of therapies in primary, secondary and tertiary level services. There can be no single blueprint for co-ordination, but a working relationship between psychological therapists in the different settings is crucial. Co-ordination might involve:

— case allocation meetings

— a central referral system

— joint clinical services for specific patient populations (e.g. abuse survivors)

— a 'brokerage' system for assessment

Today, clinical investigators have developed numerous reliable and valid measures of PTSD symptoms. Much less attention has been paid to developing psychometrically sound methods of assessing traumatic life events, which constitute the stressor criterion for a diagnosis of PTSD. This may be due in part to an assumption that extreme stressors such as combat, rape, and disasters are of such overwhelming magnitude and unequivocally universal in impact that the assessment task consists of simply establishing that an individual has experienced such an event. It has become increasingly clear, however, that such an assumption is untenable.

There is a growing recognition that traumatic stress is a complex, multifaceted construct and that its assessment entails considerable conceptual ambiguity and practical difficulty. Many investigators have called for a multidimensional approach to the assessment of traumatic life events, and new, more sophisticated instruments are beginning to emerge in response to this demand.

Several investigators have recently characterized the available instruments for assessing Criterion A events as inadequate and have proposed guidelines for the development of new assessment strategies and more useful instruments. Although specific suggestions vary, several general themes can be discerned. These themes echo some of the central issues emerging from the vast literature on the assessment of stressful life events, and the effort to develop better measures of traumatic stressors could clearly benefit from the accumulated wisdom of more than fifty years of research on "ordinary" stressors.

These general themes can be divided into conceptual issues and instrumentation issues. Conceptual issues include:

(a) the difficulty in arriving at a clear definition of trauma;

(b) the assessment of multiple dimensions of trauma, including both objective aspects and subjective appraisals;

(c) concerns about confounding objective and subjective dimensions;

(d) the assessment of traumatic events across the lifespan; and

(e) the assessment of a broad range of stressful events, including both high- and low-magnitude stressors.

Instrumentation issues include:

(a) the relative merits of questionnaires or checklists versus interviews, especially with respect to time and resources, the use of memory cueing techniques to facilitate recall, and the assessment of complex dimensions of events;

(b) the need for a clinically sensitive format;

(c) the need for direct and indirect opportunities to endorse traumatic events, including the use of both open-ended and behaviourally specific questions;

(d) reliability, including interrater and test-retest reliability;

(e) content validity, or the issue of whether items adequately assess key as-pects of traumatic events; and

(f) construct validity, including the relationship between trauma exposure and outcome variables such as PTSD symptoms as well as the often-neglected question of whether reported events can be corroborated by external sources.

A significant obstacle to the reliable and valid assessment of trauma is the almost exclusive reliance on respondents' retrospective report of their traumatic experiences. Several factors may account for inconsistencies in reports of traumatic experiences. Some respondents report more traumatic events in the second interview than in the first. This may be due to a priming effect, resulting in increased recall, or to a greater comfort level with the interview process, resulting in increased disclosure. Interviewer characteristics such as gender also may affect disclosure. It is important to note that although respondents occasionally comment on and explain the change in their report, it often is impossible to distinguish between increased recall and increased disclosure - all that is evident is the increased level of reporting.

Conversely, some respondents can report fewer events in the second interview. This may be due to simple forgetting, to an avoidance of painful emotions elicited in the first interview, or to impatience with the interview process and a desire to finish more quickly. With regard to validity, a crucial question is whether reported memories of traumatic events accurately correspond to actual events. In order to establish the degree of correspondence between reported and actual events, researchers are typically forced to rely on indirect or unreliable sources of corroboration.

Attempting to obtain adequate corroboration for reported traumatic events can be a painstaking and difficult task that all too often yields little satisfying evidence. For example, military records may only partially reflect an individual's combat experiences. It may be that costly and time-consuming longitudinal studies are the only way to adequately evaluate the correspondence between the actual events and their retrospective recall.

Although the field thus far has not developed the ideal instrument, a growing number of instruments incorporate solutions to at least some of the issues described above. In choosing an instrument, individual investigators should consider the population being assessed, the purpose of the assessment, and the time and personnel resources available. Instruments designed for assessing single or focused types of trauma are described first, followed by a few instruments designed to assess a wide range of traumatic events.

Warzone Exposure

Warzone exposure is one of the most widely studied types of trauma. Most of the available measures were developed for male Vietnam veterans, although adaptations have been made for male veterans from other conflicts. Watson et al. recently reviewed the psychometric data for five such scales. Warzone measures range widely in length and scope. One of the most utilized and well-validated is the seven-item Combat Exposure Scale. At the other extreme is the more-than 100-item survey measure employed in the National Vietnam Veterans Readjustment Study. Using this measure, King et al. identified multiple dimensions of warzone stress, including traditional combat, malevolent environment, atrocities, and perceived threat.

Childhood Trauma

Apart from combat, one of the most active areas of trauma assessment is the retrospective examination of childhood physical and sexual abuse in adults. Numerous questionnaires and interviews are available for both clinical and research purposes, although few have any psychometric validation. Some of the available measures assess a broad range of experiences, from traumas such as physical and sexual abuse to lower-magnitude stressors such as loss and familial neglect. Generally absent from these instruments is any assessment of exposure to community or street violence.

In both measures, a wide variety of questions and the use of continuous rating scales help quantify the extent of perceived stress. Many inter-views also are available, several of which have some reli-ability and validity data. The Familial Experiences Inventory provides comprehensive coverage of intrafamilial trauma and yields data on the frequency, severity, duration, and impact of each traumatic event. Reliability was variable, but was highest for items that described specific events as compared to the measurement of impact, age, and severity.

The Retrospective Assessment of Traumatic Experiences assesses parental separation and loss as well as child abuse experiences. Desirable features of the RATE include the assessment of severity of trauma based on frequency, intensity, and duration, and the inclusion of items to measure extrafamilial abuse. The National Center for PTSD is developing an as-yet-unpublished interview that comprehensively assesses childhood trauma. The Early Trauma Inventory, developed by Dudley Blake, Julie Kriegler, Lisa Zaidi, Doug Bremner, and others, combines narrative and structured approaches to inquiring about childhood emotional, physical, and sexual abuse, as well as non-abusive traumas. Each subsection begins with open-ended questioning, and then asks in detail about traumatic events.

Information is gathered about perpetrator, victim age, and frequency across three developmental periods. The respondent's appraisal of the impact of each type of trauma is assessed for both the time of occurrence and currently. Adult physical and sexual assault. Generally, most instruments in this domain assume that assault victims are women. One of the first and most widely studied questionnaires assessing partner abuse is the Conflict Tactics Scale.

Many variations on the CTS have attempted to address criticisms of the scale, including the Abusive Behaviour Inventory, which has reasonable reliability and validity. Although similar to the CTS, the ABI incorporates dimensions such as physical injury, and also assesses psychological abuse or terrorism without physical force. Another questionnaire, the Sexual Experiences Survey, assesses general sexual experiences. The SES categorizes adult sexual aggression and sexual victimization in college samples and has good one week test-retest reliability.

Torture

The Harvard Trauma Questionnaire is a self-report scale that assesses a range of torture experiences as well as PTSD and other psychiatric symptoms. It is notable for its detailed coverage of the domain of torture, including an open-ended section where respondents describe their worst experiences. In addition to events they experienced, respondents also discuss torture events they witnessed or heard about. Overall reliability was reasonable, although there was an increase in reporting of some events in the second administration.

Currently, few published instruments exist that comprehensively assess trauma across the lifespan, and it is recognized that it may not be necessary or practical to always collect this extensive and comprehensive information. Nonetheless, the lack of instrumentation is unfortunate, as the importance of assessing the occurrence of multiple types of traumas across an individual's lifetime has been increasingly emphasized in the literature. Recent research suggests that the effect of traumatic exposure may be cumulative, that trauma survivors presenting for a recent trauma are likely to have a complex prior trauma history, and that prior trauma increases the impact of current trauma.

The Traumatic Stress Schedule is a brief screening interview that asks about a range of traumatic events, including several dimensions of each endorsed event. It is designed for use by lay interviewers and it appears to have good reliability. It is important to note, however, that each of eight classes of trauma are assessed by means of a single question, and thus many traumatic events may be missed. An unusually comprehensive structured interview is the Potential Stressor Experiences Inventory, one of the most recent instruments developed by Kilpatrick, Resnick, and colleagues.

The PSEI measures lifetime exposure to a comprehensive range of trauma types and is characterized by attention both to clinical sensitivity and structured data collection. It is especially noteworthy for its use in the DSM-IV Field Trial Studies of PTSD. The PSEI assesses both low- and high-magnitude stressors, as well as objective and subjective dimensions of the first, most recent, and worst high-magnitude events.

Traumatic Stress Disorder

Accordingly, the mapping of the early responses to traumatic events has recently focused on the challenge of identifying risk factors for developing prolonged stress disorders, and in particular post-traumatic stress disorder. Early therapeutic interventions have equally been evaluated, and sanctioned, by their preventive long-term effects. Yet, the attempts to identify predictors of PTSD and to implement early preventive interventions has so far yielded limited results.

One reason for such shortcoming might be an inappropriate shift of the field of observation from examining the obvious (i.e., the inherent reasons for reacting one way or another) to exploring and manipulating elusive risk factors, such as symptoms that may be predictive of PTSD. At this point in time, therefore, there is a need and a reason to re-evaluate the early responses to traumatic events in their proper context.

The morphology (i.e., the overt expression) of early responses to traumatic events has been repeatedly described. Yet there seems to be little agreement about the nature of these responses. For example, the early distressful responses to traumatic events have been construed as both 'pathogenic' and 'normal' in the sense of being (a) a risk factor for developing of PTSD and, at the same time (b) a necessary step towards recovery. To make the problem worse, specific symptoms, such as dissociation, intrusive recall of the event and early depression have been conceived as 'pathogenic'.

All the same, almost everyone is perturbed during the aftermath of a trauma, and everyone experiences a degree of intrusive recall and sadness. Alternatively, better understanding might be gained from looking at the adaptive role of behaviour emitted at the aftermath of traumatic events. The following enclosure offers a short formulation of this approach, specifically addressing the adaptive value of early PTSD 'symptoms.' An important function of the early response is communication. Outcry is universally emitted in situations of pain, forced separation and distress.

Recruiting support from co-species, signaling one's position upon forced separation and, in general, communicating distress to helping others are extremely useful survival-related behaviors. Yet, like most emitted signals, the ultimate outcome of such behaviour depends on its ability to elicit appropriate responses from others and make use of such responses. Continuous expressions of distress may, therefore, reflect either a failure to elicit proper responses or a failure to use it appropriately.

The multiple dimensions of a 'trauma' Another problematic point is the erroneous assertion that traumatic stressors are distinguished by the presence of a threat, as exemplified by the current definition of a traumatic event by DSM IV. Following are the traumatizing elements of extreme events:

— Threat
— Physiological strain (pain, starvation, dehydration)
— Exhaustion
— Surrender
— Separation
— Relocation
— Loss

— Isolation

— Dehumanization

— Uncertainty

— Incongruent experience

— Exposure to the grotesque

Few of these terms require detailed explanation, yet they significantly shape the early responses. Loss can be concrete or symbolic (beliefs and expectations). Loss may also involve social networks, community structures, financial and personal resources. Relocation is an assault on a deeply embedded territorial habit of humans. It uproots people from cherished land, familiar environment, dear objects and reassuring life routines. Isolation (e.g., during captivity) violates a profound need of humans to share the company of others.

Importantly, mental isolation may occur even when others are present. Feeling disconnected, detached and unable to resonate with others is a salient description of many traumatized survivors. Dehumanization and degradation (e.g., as prisoner or war, during sexual assault or group rape) leave severe psychological scars beyond those engendered by threat. This is particularly true when surrender and obedience are enforced. Uncertainty during traumatic events (e.g., as to the duration or the source of adversity) is often depicted as extremely distressful.

Finally, incongruence, that is, the absolute novelty of an experience and its salient contrast with what had been believed in, known, expected or experienced beforehand is probably the most difficult part of the trauma for many survivors. Examples of the above include the responses of trained rescue workers to being exposed to body parts of young children; of a survivor of sadistic rape who reported having been faced with evil; of a wounded soldier who, during air - evacuation was exposed to the agonizing screams of a friend and ultimately to his death. Holocaust survivors coined the name 'the other planet' to describe Auschwitz.

Scholars of the Vietnam War spoke of a psychological 'trauma membrane' separating what had been experienced 'there' from the rest of their lives. These terms epitomize the idea of incongruent experiences and properly place them at the core of mental traumatization. Responses are 'polymorphous and labile' Given the variety of traumatic experiences it is clear that, according to circumstances, survivors' responses may involve apprehension, anger, bewilderment, grief, regret, yearning, attempts to retrieve and repair, efforts to control emotions, attempt to forget, and attempts to reappraise and make sense of what has just happened.

Empirical studies of the early responses reveal these to be "polymorphous and labile," that is, changing rapidly and including a mixture of anxiety, depression, agitation, stupor, numbing and irritability. Grinker and Spiegel describe the early 'neurotic' response as consisting of "a passing parade of every type of psychological and psychosomatic symptom." Whilst the 'heterogeneity' or 'polymorphism' can baffle researchers the experience of those who rescue trauma survivors is very different.

Rather than being erratic and incomprehensible to the intimate observer, early responses are eminently and intuitively understandable. They are also very communicative, and readily evoke intense emotional responses and enduring impressions in helpers. Indeed, they rapidly create intense and mutual bonding between rescuer and survivors. Therefore, the early responses are clearly understandable, especially when one is ready to read human faces and respond to human emotion.

Emotional reading, a deeply embedded function of the human brain offers one of the best approaches to 'mapping the multidimensional picture' of the acute response to traumatic events. Along the same line, the 'lability' of the early responses is also understandable. Intuitively we know that the response to traumatic should change with time, from an initial 'outcry' to subsequent phases of mourning and elaboration. Yet, the proper time unit here is 'psychological time,' and the latter may differ from one individual to another.

Moreover, the sequence of responses may be different in different individuals, with some being initially shut down and unexpressive, and opening up later, and others reacting in very expressive ways - to be soothed with time. When one evaluates groups of survivors, the differences in personal timing, inner experiences, personal and cultural style almost invariably yields a 'labile and polymorphous' picture. Much better understanding may be gained from following individual paths. Indeed, a single observation can hardly inform us about the quality and complexities of an individual's response.

Finally, the period that follows a traumatic event is not uneventful. Secondary stressors (e.g., relocation; disclosing rape experience, enduring surgical operations) tend to follow the primary ones. These new stressors evoke new responses and, as will be argued below, send the survivor, who may already be in a phase of learning and reappraisal, back to fighting for survival.

The impact phase of a traumatic event is characterized by actual presence of adversity. Despite the use of the word 'impact' this period can be of various duration.

Importantly, primary stress responses are seen at this stage, and these responses are often very powerful, unexpected and take control of a person's behaviour. Survivors, therefore, often find themselves acting in ways that they did not expect and had no previous experience of. For example, threatened by likely death a rape victim may surrender her body. A young father may escape from a burning house, leaving a child behind. A soldier may find himself paralyzed by fear while others launch an attack. To the extent that these acts are 'out of character' or 'out of one's repertoire' these very early responses will be revisited later during the phase of reappraisal when self criticism may be harsh and condemning.

During the impact phase survivors primarily require protection from adversity. This, however, may not always be possible because the adverse effect of some events continue (e.g., when one's child is missing following a disaster). Even during prolonged adversities to is possible for, adequate help to reduce the randomness of the situation as well as the survivor's helplessness and loneliness. The main role of helpers at this stage can be equated with that of a 'primary organizer,' that is, a person who, by his or her stable presence reduces the randomness of both external and internal realities.

Construct of Coping

'Coping' is the psychological and behavioural correlate of the bodily efforts to maintain its inner milieu within viable (or homeostatic) boundaries despite excessive demands. By analogy, coping with stress is an effort to maintain psychological balance and functioning despite excessive demands. Coping theorists describe a broad range of mechanisms designed to 'increase the gap between stress and distress.' Such 'coping strategies' are generally divided into 'problem-focused,' 'emotional-focused' and 'appraisal-related'.

Individuals are said to have specific 'coping styles'. That is they engage in a typical mixture of tactics when faced with stress. Some individuals tend to prefer action to reflection; others are preferentially help-seekers, yet others tend to be emotional and expressive. Studies of trauma survivors have mainly addressed the effectiveness of particular coping strategies.

Among combat veterans, Solomon et al, for example, found the use of emotion-focused and blunting coping strategies to be associated with higher levels of psychiatric symptoms whereas problem-focussed strategies lead to a decrease in symptoms. A survivor is coping better when he or she experiences relatively controllable emotions, can continue the task at hand (e.g., seeking shelter, reviewing his or her nightmares), keeps a sense of self-worth and, most importantly, engages in rewarding communication.

Traumatic events certainly disrupt a person's sense of coping and therefore lead to temporary periods in which individuals may be flooded by distress, feelings of worthlessness and may be unable to make use of help offered. This is not by any means true for all survivors nor for all stages of the response. For some survivors the impact phase may involve paralyzing fear, disrupted behaviour and a sense of total chaos. For others, however, the rescue period can be extremely difficult despite having coped well during the impact phase (e.g., when bad news is brought).

Finally, and most importantly, the long-term effect of traumatic events is significantly affected by the way in which found an advantage to accrue from avoidance, denial and receiving group support. Spurrell and McFarlane found no clear advantage of any coping strategy. These conflicting results should not surprise us, because it might be true that achieving effective coping is more important than any particular strategy In order to succeed one's coping must match the circumstances of the event and the survivor's resources. These in turn differ between events, within events (e.g., at different stages) and between individuals.

Surrender, stoic acceptance and cognitive re-framing may be more appropriate to situations in which the stressor is uncontrollable (e.g., captivity) whereas action to reduce the stressor, or help seeking are more appropriate in other circumstances. The idea of evaluating coping efficacy has distinct advantages for understanding the early responses to traumatic events. Regardless of the type of trauma, the stage of the response sequence a person is in or the task to be accomplished successful coping will affect the survivor in a very typical way.

Pearlin and Schooler suggested four observable consequences of effective coping:

(a) relief of distress,

(b) sense of personal worth,

(c) ability to enjoy rewarding interpersonal contacts, and

(d) sustained task performance.

Ineffective coping will lead to impaired task performance, uncontrollable emotions, self-blame (or worthlessness) and inability to enjoy the presence of others. Instead, coping may involve contingent (yet more controllable) stressors as well as one's own responses. In a study of survivors of a terrorist attack, Shalev et al described various coping efforts used during the impact phase. These included actively rescuing other survivors, sharing important information with the rescuers, preserving one's dignity by covering one's body or controlling the disclosure of information about the event to one's relatives. Successfully achieving such individual goals increased the survivors' sense of control and reduced their distress face a new reality.

For instance, evacuees find themselves in a shelter; injured survivors in hospital; released hostages may be on their way home. Importantly the new reality is also psychological. Having survived a sadistic assault a person's internal reality is very different - but not yet shaped in any specific way. Typically, at this stage one has to face the new reality without having changed internally. Hence, it is the old self which struggles with a new reality; often with a great amount of confusion and bewilderment.

This process is referred to as 'accommodation,' in the sense that existing resources are used and extended to cope with novelty. The prevalent feeling is that the world is not the same. Yet the intensity and the pervasiveness of the experience differ between survivors. Importantly, this feeling of alienation and of major (and negative) change may remain with the survivor and become part of his or her prolonged response to the trauma. The role of helpers at this stage is to mitigate the novelty of the situation such that survivors are not totally estranged and alienated.

In other words, the presence and the warmth of helpers, as well as their somewhat better capacity to endure emotions, provide the necessary 'holding' for distraught survivors. Indeed this is the stage where people are often observed to hug one another. It is also important to acknowledge that helpers can function as effective 'holders' to the extent that they are assisted and supported themselves for instance by being part of a team.

Most will repeatedly, vividly and involuntarily recall the traumatic event through intrusive thoughts and images, nightmares and flashbacks. Many will share these experiences with others for instance by repeating their story again and again. Others may think that they are going mad because of the unusualness of the intrusive and vivid images and memories. Negative appraisal of one's early symptoms increases the likelihood of subsequent PTSD. At this phase survivors are psychologically assimilating their recent experiences, try to understand its meaning and examine key learning points relevant taking account of previous life experiences and future expectations.

This is properly the 'post-traumatic' period, during which the concrete event becomes a mental event. Optimally, the new experience can be assimilated and this is likely to be reflected in subtle yet consistent changes in the survivor's appraisal the circumstances of the event and of his or her feelings and actions. Dreams become more detailed with elements from one's past appearing alongside representations of the traumatic event. The telling of the story becomes a conversation. Other pieces of information, (e.g., observations made by others, references to options and choices, links with past experiences) can be brought in and accepted.

The traumatic event can thereby becomes a formative event. There is a sense of being changed, but not of being torn apart. Survivors differ in the extent to which they tolerate the necessary phase of intrusive recall. For some, nightmares are a dreadful experience and recall is fearfully avoided. The story is never told, may be truncated, reduced or even schematized and repeated without change. Importantly, nothing changes with time. Converstions about the traumatic event is avoided because 'no one can understand', including oneself. Memories remain fragmented, iconic, poorly verbalized. Negative perception of self and others generalize and extend to other events and people. A sense of radical unwelcome transformations prevails.

The traumatic event becomes destructive life experience. It is during this period that a stable narrative of the traumatic events and of one's own responses to it are formed and consolidated. The narrative, however, is never purely an individual creation, but rather includes elements of what has been said by others and of the larger social appraisal of the event. The resulting mixture of personal experience and adopted facts may consolidate into a set of memories that will later be remembered as 'authentic' and 'accurate'.

4

Types of Therapeutic Practices

The term psychiatric treatment covers all therapeutic approaches used in children with emotional and behavioural disturbances. Specific types of treatment can be divided into psychological therapies and physical therapies.

- Psychological:
  - Behavioural
  - Cognitive behavioural
  - Psychodynamic, psychoanalytic.
- Physical:
  - Medication
  - Diet.

Psychological Therapies

Psychological therapies are termed behavioural if they aim to alter what the child or family do by methods that tackle the symptoms directly, without consideration of thoughts or feelings. For example, a specific phobia may be successfully treated by a desensitisation programme directed toward gradual familiarisation with the feared object in imagination or in real life.

Cognitive behavioural therapy aims to produce behavioural change by relating maladaptive patterns of thinking to behaviour, and cognitive therapy focuses exclusively on changing maladaptive thoughts. For example, depressive states may be maintained by false ideas about the way other people think about the patient. These may be influenced by encouraging the child to record the circumstances in which these thoughts occur and checking whether their beliefs are justified.

Psychological therapies also include those that aim to uncover underlying conflicts, tensions, and drives of which the child and family members were previously unaware and which are thought to be the covert source of the problem. For example, an anxiety state may have developed because the child has aggressive feelings toward a sibling that they have repressed and are unaware of until these feelings are uncovered by therapy. This may involve observing, listening, and talking or playing with the child.

Such insight promoting therapies are termed psychoanalytic if they are clearly derived from the work of early psychoanalysts, especially Sigmund and Anna Freud and Melanie Klein. The term psychoanalytic treatment is usually reserved for quite intensive individual treatment, and it is more likely to be termed psychotherapy or psychodynamic therapy if the underlying concepts are the same but treatment is provided on a less frequent basis. Much of once weekly or less frequent counselling uses a similar framework.

However, psychological therapies can also be classified according to the unit (individual, family, or group) to which therapy is applied. Those engaged in family therapy may use either psychodynamic or behavioural concepts, or a mixture of the two.. They may also use concepts that are special to family therapists. Thus, systems therapy is based on the notion that families can be viewed as homeostatic entities - if you change one part of the system you alter the remainder. Not so long ago there was considerable antagonism between psychodynamic therapists and behaviour therapists.

Psychodynamic therapists saw behaviourism as superficial tinkering that left the real problems untouched. Behaviourists saw psychodynamic therapists as misguidedly applying an unproven set of theories, with little interest in or evidence for success. Such mutual dismissiveness has by no means disappeared, but there is distinctly more appreciation of the fact that different forms of treatment can be valuable in different circumstances.

Physical Therapies

Physical therapies are less commonly used in children. They include medication, dietary approaches, and electroconvulsive treatment, the latter of which is used either extremely rarely or not at all until late adolescence, and even then to a rapidly diminishing degree.

Child mental health professionals also provide indirect treatment through consultation without direct clinical contact. Consultation and liaison work is carried out especially with paediatricians, social workers, and teachers.

Finally, there are various miscellaneous forms of psychiatric treatment that cannot readily be classified according to the above system. Hypnosis, for example, aims to allow the child greater control of their behaviour by means of techniques used while they are in a state of altered awareness.

Child and Adolescent Mental Health Services (CAMHS) is increasingly becoming the generic term. Child and adolescent departments of psychiatry or mental health may be sited in general hospitals, psychiatric hospitals, children's hospitals, or in the community. Inpatient units usually admit either children who are from 6-7 years old up to early adolescence, or they admit older adolescents. Some units for young adults will also admit older adolescents. Inpatient units may admit a proportion of day patients, and there is a relatively small number of child psychiatric day centres exclusively given over to day patients.

Professional teams working in any of these centres are likely to be multidisciplinary, and treatment may be delivered by any of the professionals involved. Child and adolescent psychiatrists have particular skills in formulating clinical problems in which both biological and psychosocial factors are important. They are usually the gatekeepers for inpatient treatment. As well as child and adolescent psychiatrists, who are medically trained, the team is likely to include clinical psychologists.

Although traditionally psychologists have spent much time systematically testing children, they now spend a much greater proportion of their time assessing children and families, and then devising and sometimes carrying out programmes of treatment. There is increasing emphasis throughout medical practice on the need to provide treatment that is evidence based. The degree to which one can state that child psychiatric treatment is based on good evidence depends on the definition of evidence, on the particular diagnosis, and on the nature of the intervention. Before describing specific forms of therapy, it is worth remembering that all therapy will be more effective if the practitioner shows the characteristics of genuineness, trust, and empathy, which were shown 50 years ago to be essential for therapeutic success.Such features of the therapist go far to explain the success of alternative forms of therapy that are not described here because the empirical evidence for their effectiveness is lacking.

Psychological therapies are much more difficult to evaluate using controlled designs, but recently considerable progress has been made in this direction. A number of studies have been conducted in children, and this approach has been demonstrated to be effective in a variety of conditions. Thus, some young children with conduct disorders, especially if these are of mild or moderate severity, respond to parent management training.Severe conduct disorders are improved with so-called multisystem therapy. Cognitive behaviour therapy is an effective treatment for some depressive and anxiety disorders, as well as for obsessive-compulsive states and post-traumatic stress disorder. Monosymptomatic phobias respond to behavioural treatment, and the bell and pad alarm is another form of behaviour therapy that is effective in nocturnal enuresis.

Psychoanalytic psychotherapy and counselling

It is difficult to distinguish between these two approaches, but in general counselling is likely to involve a higher component of advice and guidance, with less dependence on a theoretical model involving the presence of unconscious mechanisms. Psychoanalytic psychotherapy is probably effective in some diffuse anxiety states.Family therapy has been shown to be effective in a variety of conditions.It appears, for example, to reduce the frequency of attacks in childhood asthma and, when combined with other approaches, to be an effective intervention in anorexia nervosa.

For some common disorders, it remains likely that non-specific factors such as the enthusiasm of the therapist and the motivation of family members are of greater importance than the specific type of treatment employed. Paediatricians and general practitioners in training who find themselves working with psychiatrists and psychologists with different therapeutic orientations may be confused, but should find that they can learn much that is of value from observing the application of different approaches to similar problems.

In particular, they may benefit as much from observing how child mental health professionals can clarify the nature of a problem, helping the child and family to see their difficulties in a new way, as they can from observing specific treatment interventions. As the classification systems used in child psychiatry become more refined, there will probably be increased precision in our application of different forms of treatment. In the meantime, it would be highly desirable for evaluative studies to include not only scientifically valid controlled trials but also measures of consumer satisfaction.

With increasing dependence on their "customers", among whom they must certainly count those working in primary care and paediatric settings, child mental health professionals will be increasingly sensitive to what their clients think of their interventions. Children with active suicidal thoughts or psychotic symptoms Emotional or behaviour problems not responding to first line counselling Difficult diagnostic problems with no obvious organic cause.

Children with moderately severe behaviour or emotional problems or with disabling psychosomatic symptoms should be referred to a child mental health service if the problems do not resolve after first line counselling. Children who are appreciably functionally disabled by persistent physical problems that either have no organic basis or an insufficient organic explanation need referral, and the earlier they are referred the better. Similarly, children with active suicidal thoughts or psychotic symptoms should be referred urgently.

When, in a paediatric clinic, it is clear from the time of first attendance that children presenting with difficult diagnostic problems probably have a non-organic explanation for their symptoms, then again the children should be referred early on - preferably while physical investigations are still being carried out. This is so that when all results prove negative, the child psychiatric department is not seen as a last resort or "dustbin" department.

Instead, the child psychiatrist is seen as someone who has been involved from the start. In the very occasional child who turns out to have an abdominal tumour or a degenerative neurological condition to explain, for example, severe stomach aches or headaches, the early involvement of a psychiatrist need not antagonise parents if it is made clear at the outset that the diagnostic process may indeed show an organic cause.

Therapeutic Environment

There is a body of theoretical, research and practice information pointing to core conditions that facilitate all therapy. Sometimes, these conditions are more difficult to recognize or produce than at others. The therapeutic environment what are the environmental conditions which best facilitate the therapeutic process? Major aspects of the facilitative environment are often taken for granted on the principles and techniques of unique theoretical orientations.

Drawing on extensive research and clinical practice from many theoretical perspectives, what constitutes the core conditions for facilitating therapy. Comparisons between theories attest to striking differences as well as striking commonalties. Clear and accurate descriptions of concepts and their implementation serve to highlight 'common factors', while those instances where theoretical orientation prompts divergence are specifically identified. Therapists are not automatically graced with productive therapeutic environments, no matter how advanced their training. No amount of knowledge or experience can dictate all the human factors clients and therapists bring to a given session.

Conscious planning and preparation of an environment is the starting place, but the ability to recognize and adapt to changing situations is essential follow-up. The conceptual guides and practical examples that follow are designed to aid understanding of the core facilitating conditions essential for therapeutic efficacy and to offer direction for implementing them in the real world of therapeutic practice. Perhaps the best descriptor of core conditions is that they pertain, in some general way, to conditions that promote productive interactions between therapist and client.

All therapy requires some form of connection, although we may disagree on what combination of physical (visual, tactile, olfactory, etc.), verbal, written, spiritual or other conditions are essential to promote that connection. Even though a gathering of experienced therapists would produce a wide variety of ways to visualize and deal with Kristin, research and practice confirm that each therapist would probably be successful. Somehow therapy works. The chances of Kristin being helped by an experienced therapist are quite good.

Meta-analyses of research studies on the value of psychotherapy find that from two-thirds to four-fifths of people do get better as a result of therapy. These same analyses show that the theoretical approach of a therapist does not seem to make any consistent difference. Jerome and Julia Frank probably best capture the way many professionals see these results in practice when they conclude that theories which endure rather than disappear must be doing some good or people would stop going to therapists of those theoretical orientations.

Even studies done by groups evaluating the profession from the outside have determined that therapy works. These findings are good news for the public, but they also cause headaches for therapists and educators trying to determine best techniques or even attempting to define the key factors in quality practice. What can account for consistently positive therapeutic results coming from such a wide variety of theoretical approaches?

Garfield and Bergin summarize the findings and thoughts of many in determining that there must be some common or 'nonspecific' conditions that all 'quality' therapists provide. Identifying these facilitative conditions has been difficult, but one consistent theme throughout the research is that a significant part of the answer lies within what is generally called the 'therapeutic relationship'.

Therapists who consider working with someone like Kristin have good reason to be concerned about the potential for poor outcomes. All of a therapist's training, experience and theoretical knowledge cannot make up for an environment that denies the development of productive interactions. One essential ingredient is that clients must have some capacity for a positive relationship. Those with better mental health are more likely to demonstrate this capacity and those who are making progress with a therapist tend to continue improving on this capacity and its.

In effect, it appears that the healthier clients are at the beginning of therapy or the better they become during therapy, the more likely they are to develop the necessary therapeutic relationships. The same research shows that therapists have the ability to improve the positive relationship capacity of their clients. Emphasizing behaviours that focus on the relationship between client and therapist seems to be the general way that such a positive relational environment is promoted.

Dealing with client defences, guilt and problematic feelings towards the therapist are all effective measures a therapist can take. Therapists may not be able to control the entire relational environment, but it appears that they must at least work towards a point where the relationship is 'good enough' to be therapeutic. Kristin brings much less capacity for positive relationships than a therapist might like. The question is, does she bring enough to begin making progress? Her therapist must somehow judge this potential and then behave in ways that create a facilitative environment where a more productive relationship can evolve.

Theory, practice and research each provide their own pieces of information on the dimensions of a facilitative environment that help direct what therapists can do to maximize the potential for a positive therapeutic relationship and thus therapeutic success. The information available on the connection between facilitative environment - in particular, the therapeutic relationship - and successful therapy is multidimensional. Each dimension provides a separate focus and details that must first be considered individually to make them clear and useful as part of the whole. No single dimension fully controls the relationship, although differing views of theory, research and practice apportion widely varying importance to the different factors involved.

Conditions that produce some form of involvement are needed between client and therapist for the therapist to take partial responsibility for any positive developments. Being physically in the same room is the common contact for most therapies, but even that is challenged by increasing numbers of professionals who are doing therapy over the telephone or Internet. Moderate temperature and lighting, comfortable sitting or reclining opportunities rather than standing and minimized distracting noises, clutter and interruptions are found in virtually any successful therapist's room.

These essentials are so much a part of the professional atmosphere that they are virtually taken for granted in textbooks and research. Yet theoretical differences regarding the physical foundations of therapy already begin to emerge within these basic boundaries.

The classical analyst has a client/patient lie on a couch, unable to see the therapist so that the client's thinking might be relatively uninfluenced by the therapist's physical presence. Gestalt therapists, at the other end of the spectrum, consider essential therapeutic ingredients to be close, face-to-face, person-to-person, even physical contact. Each theory thus has its own unique view of what physical behaviours are appropriate in relation to the purpose, techniques and goals of therapy.

All therapies attend to emotions. The difference is in the value placed on emotions and their role in therapy. Person-centred therapists attend directly to client emotions as a vehicle for understanding the unique aspects of their phenomenological worlds. Their belief is that logic, reason, history, and so on, used alone draw attention away from the most unique experiences of clients, while emotions are more likely to highlight these important aspects.

Most cognitive therapists, on the other hand, advocate that thought, logic and illogic control emotions and that the emphasis of therapy should therefore be on those 'rational' processes. Similarly, classical behavioural therapists will use learning and training to change emotions, which they see as being little more than secondary markers of behaviours.

Society and cultures imbue therapists and clients with expectations that must be given attention for therapy to succeed. White Europeans and Americans have had the greatest influence on the development. The therapeutic environment of most therapeutic/counselling theories. Katz summarizes this fact by stating, 'similarities between white culture and cultural values that form the foundations of traditional counselling theory and practice exist and are interchangeable'. Feminist and multicultural criticisms of these theories are generally based on the concept that not everyone fits this male, Euro-American worldview.

Asian cultures, for example, would place more value on the family or group identity than on individuality. Females also tend to take a more collaborative approach to life than males. On a societal level, some would encourage therapists to report anyone with anti-government thinking, while others would see even plotting and planning as therapeutically private issues unless they were likely to physically harm someone. These few examples highlight the need to take cultural factors into consideration in developing a facilitative environment.

What people think, how they arrive at those thoughts and what they can do about them take up much of the time and energy in the therapeutic environment. Questions about people's ability to think or style of thinking need to be considered, since theories vary on the extent and type of thinking necessary. Dealing with ambiguity and abstractions are essentials for the client in existential therapy, whereas the same client working with a behavioural therapist would be given much more simplistic and concrete thinking tasks. Adlerians, on the other hand, would ask clients to do substantial memory work about their childhood with the expectation that such memories could and would be recalled.

Some theories presume that sufficient recall of information and perceptions are available in the conscious mind for therapy to work. Others spend more time attempting to illuminate the unconscious with the belief that key therapeutic factors are not available to simple conscious recall. Techniques used vary between therapists as they view the thinking process and abilities of their clients differently, even though they all attend to the importance of the thinking variable in one way or another.

The past provides the greatest number of actual events for consideration in therapy. The present provides the most immediately available and tangible events. The future holds the much-desired, imagined. Somehow therapy works 11 events that might constitute a better existence, although there is nothing concrete or observable about them. All theories attend to each of these three time frames in their own ways, while they also have different priorities as to which frame deserves greater attention.

The 'here-and-now' focus of gestalt and other humanistic oriented therapies demonstrate an orientation to therapy that emphasizes immediate interaction and change. What is done is done and what will happen in the future is fully dependent on what we do now. So concentrate on the present. In contrast, psychodynamic and behavioural therapists, who disagree on many areas, both emphasize that the present is built upon the past.

Common to all therapies, though, is the assumption that an improved future results from some change occurrence. One problem that arises when considering core facilitative conditions is differentiating between the conditions and actions that produce a facilitative environment, and the therapeutic techniques that require such an environment in order to be effective.

Psychotherapy of Opioid Dependence

In developing responses to opioid dependence there is a need to clarify the scale of the problems that have to be tackled, the currently available resources utilized in responding and the evidence for the efficacy of currently used or currently available interventions. The needs assessment exercise aims to ensure.that an identified problem and a clearly defined means of responding to it are organized so that resources are used as effectively as possible.

The actual cultural setting will also have a major influence on what is and what is not an acceptable form of treatment irrespective of the evidence on the efficacy of the treatment. The cultural acceptability and sensitivity to cultural issues is a critical part of the overall approach to community consultation and community engagement and involvement as part of the service development. Problems to be tackled:

— Polysubstance use
— Injecting drug use
— Associated transmission of HIV and other blood-borne infections
— Chronic health problems
— Social exclusion
— Personal / Social functioning
— Crime involvement

The initial focus is usually on long term residential and drug free rehabilitation as the key part of the service response to opioid dependence. However in many countries, as the scale of the problem grows and access is required for substantial populations, then consideration is given to developing more affordable and accessible community based treatments.

The increasing focus into community based treatments with involvement of broad generic health and social welfare resources enables broader community involvement. The challenge for the coming decade is to fashion public health based treatment systems for drug dependence that can enable a broad range of prevention and treatment interventions to be targeted at the 'at risk' population. This should reduce the risks associated with this pattern of drug use and maximize the numbers who return to a fully functioning role in society. There is a need for clarity of aims and objectives of treatments. When these have been made clear and the goal of the treatment is clearly set, it should be possible to measure these objectives while treatment is being delivered.

Over a twenty-year period it is estimated that a heroin addict has the same chance of managing to stop using drugs as they have of dying from drug use. About one third die, one third manage to stop and the other third continue a long battle with their addiction, including time in prison, time in treatment and time on the street. In the long term many continue using heroin persistently into their middle age and beyond. Because of the chronic nature of heroin addiction and the repeated use of local health services, health practitioners came to realize that methadone maintenance could provide major stability and improvement for those who were continuing drug use despite abstinence-oriented treatment.

The method of maintenance agonist pharmacotherapy is controversial and initially unappealing. However, in the face of the range of options and following extensive and repeated experimental trials there is now a high level of consensus on the efficacy of this form of treatment. The advent of HIV and AIDS added a new degree of urgency to finding structured ways of responding to injecting drug use in the community and has spurred many countries to rapidly expand methadone maintenance treatment as part of the HIV prevention strategy.

This type of treatment is no magic bullet. In regular practice it achieves moderately modest outcomes but systematic reviews indicate that these are significant treatment effects and it is judged that these treatment effects are cost effective and practical in the face of the limited alternative options. Treatment outcome expectations:

— Elimination or at least reduction of illicit opiate and other drug use
— Reduction in risk of infectious diseases
— Improved physical and psychological health
— Improved social functioning
— Reintegration into society
— Reduction in criminal behaviour

Marsch, from a meta-analysis of studies, concluded that methadone maintenance treatment has a moderate but significant effect on illicit opiate use and a small to moderate effect on HIV risk behaviours. In terms of overall criminal behaviour, methadone maintenance treatment was found to have a small to moderate effect but when analyzed in terms of type of crime, methadone maintenance treatment was found to have a significant and large effect on drug-related criminal behaviour.

The Treatment Outcomes Prospective Study (TOPS) found that retention in treatment at three months was highest for methadone maintenance treatment, followed by therapeutic communities and outpatient drug-free treatment. In terms of reductions in drug use and criminality, methadone maintenance treatment and therapeutic communities were equally effective. But these were naturalistic studies where patients chose their own treatment modality.

The three major US large-scale outcome studies, conducted over the last three decades respectively DARP, TOPS and DATOS all reported similar positive findings using methadone maintenance with major reductions in the key outcome domains of drug use, criminality and risk taking behaviour. The English NTORS evaluation of the treatment of Drug Dependence during the 1990s, also reported similar positive findings for both residential drug free treatment and methadone based treatment in the community, at five year follow up.

Among heroin users attending public treatment centers in Italy, the retention rate after one year was 40% for methadone maintenance treatment, 18% for naltrexone, and 15% for drug-free treatment. Over the past decade there have been a number of studies aimed at developing alternative long acting opioid agonists that could be used for opioid agonist maintenance pharmacotherapy. Buprenorphine, which is a μ-receptor partial agonist and LAAM (levo-alpha-acetyl-methadol) have been most extensively assessed. Buprenorphine has been used in many settings especially in Europe. Both medications appear to be comparable in efficacy to methadone and there are both advantages and disadvantages to the differing medications.

Internatioal Perspectives and Role of Pharmacotherapy

There has been a major expansion in the provision of opioid maintenance treatment in the European Union over the past decade. One of the key drives behind this expansion has been concern about HIV and concerted efforts to contain the spread of HIV among injecting drug users. After an initial epidemic spread there is reasonable evidence that HIV infection among injecting drug users has been significantly contained over the past five years. No single intervention can account for this, but the provision of a broad range of treatments including drug substitution treatment has been an important component of this result.

Most countries in the EU have seen a down turn in new infections and a downturn in the incidence of AIDS, however the reduction in incidence of HIV/AIDS may be related to development of new anti-retroviral treatment agents. Overall there is consensus that the broad range of interventions including educational, prevention, and treatment approaches has had an impact on the range of risk taking behaviour in injecting drug users. After an initial spread of HIV among injecting drug users in countries such as Italy, Spain, France and Ireland, major public health progress has been made towards reducing the spread of HIV among injecting drug users.

Other countries such as the Netherlands, UK, Sweden and Denmark have had low levels of HIV among injecting drug users and have continued to maintain these low levels. To date it is safe to say that the containment of the spread of HIV among injecting drug users in the European Union has been one of the more successful results of current drug policy. The experience has been similar in Australia where the development of a broad and comprehensive range of treatments including extensive provision of methadone maintenance has been very successful in containing HIV spread among injecting drug users.

The containment of hepatitis, and in particular hepatitis C, to date has not been as successful and presents a major public health challenge for the coming decade. It is estimated that the base line prevalence in many countries is very high and that this virus appears to be more transmissible for a variety of factors. One of the other key challenges for the public health of these populations has been the high mortality associated with drug injecting use and opioid dependence.

There is good evidence that treatment significantly reduces the mortality rates compared with those not in treatment, and substitution treatment has been demonstrated to significantly reduce mortality also. This has been difficult to demonstrate at the population level because of differing ways of collecting and recording deaths in different countries.

Opium use spread to India and then to China, but was mainly used for purposes of medication. In Greece, opium was used by medical priests who regarded it as a metaphysical substance. However, Hippocrates, the founder of modern medicine, dissociated himself from the magical attributes of opium, realizing that it should be used sparingly and emphasizing the risk of habituation.

In Roman times, the poppy was seen as a powerful symbol of sleep and death. It was used as a method for murder and suicide and became an important classical theatre symbol with all its attendant terror. Opium reached China by the 8th century. By the 9th century, Arab physicians were publishing texts on 'afyum' (opium), and reporting on its medicinal qualities.

The Arab physicians were the most scholarly and advanced and were servants to the powers of the time. Doctors and scholars promoted the role of opium and its growth in international trade along with herbs, spices and other related exotic goods. Although the opium trade grew, it was very small then in comparison with modern day trafficking. Nevertheless, traders had identified it as a useful commodity.

McCoy, reports that it was not until the 15 th century that opium became a regular item of intra-Asian trade with the Persians and Indians having some use for it as a recreational euphoria producing substance. The great seafaring traders of Medieval.times expanded the opium trade, firstly through the Venetians and subsequently through the Portuguese, Dutch, British and French colonists. Acosta recorded the condemnation of opium by Arabic, Persian, Turkish and Indian, Malay, Chinese and Malabar doctors, who all decried the drug for its risk of habituation.

The Portuguese attempted to compete with the Chinese and import opium from Western India into China, but with limited success. However, they did identify the opium trade as an important source of revenue. Subsequently, the Dutch entered into the trade with a more aggressive and competitive manner and established control in the Dutch East Indies. The Dutch East India Company imported large amounts of opium for sale to the Indonesian and Javanese populations and opium became one of the most traded commodities and a major source of revenue.

The British followed with the establishment of the British East India Company in 1656 and the trade was to develop even more over the next fifty years and continued for another hundred and thirty years. This policy gave rise to two Opium Wars as a result of Chinese opposition to the trade, and created a vast population of opium addicts in China estimated at 10% of the adult population. This opium was produced in Bengal and its sale was controlled by the Colonial Administration and the East India Company. Opium chests were smuggled into China by clipper ships with large traders dominating the market.

After the second Opium War, the Chinese legalized the opium trade but kept control of the customs duty and regulated the domestic trade. This resulted in a considerable growth in opium production in China itself with Szechwan and Yunnan being the main producer provinces. Subsequently, Yunnan became a net producer and exporter of opium using mule trains to cross the mountains into Siam, Burma, and French Indo-China. The Chinese population developed very high rates of opioid dependence. McCoy, reports that during the nineteenth century, state licensed opium dens became a unique South East Asian institution, spreading and sustaining opiate use throughout the region.

The 1990s saw an explosion of illicit drug use and dependence in the region. Global structural changes have influenced local trends such as the opening up of economic structures to improve the flow of trade between countries. The evolution of drug related problems in society are complex and cannot be explained by any simple or single cause. However, it is fair to say that after a period of relative containment there is now a rapid growth in the number of heroin users in the region and also a rapid growth in the number of psycho-stimulant users.

The issues of HIV prevention and HIV spread continue to be a major challenge in the South East Asia and Western Pacific regions. Despite some notable successes in prevention campaigns, the overall trends in the region indicate ongoing major HIV spread. Part of the challenge is to address the substantial social, cultural and economic changes that are taking place with social upheaval, economic reform and new channels of global communication having an effect. The phenomenon of globalization has affected young peoples' social behaviour and life style expectations. Changes in sexual behaviour in many countries provide a considerable risk for the spread of heterosexual HIV among the general population.

For some time it has been recognized that the young drug using and drug injecting population is a potentially significant bridgehead for the spread of HIV into the heterosexual community. Different virus subtypes tend to spread among different sub-populations. The study of these phenomena in Thailand has shown that there is considerable mixing of these different subtypes, partially amongst sex workers being involved in injecting drug use but also from infected drug injectors having unprotected sex with sex workers.

All countries have a national strategy and a range of legislative and control approaches to the drugs problem. Structural reforms in the public health sector, with particular reference to mechanisms for financing and organizing health care, are a particular challenge in many countries. The issue of resourcing responses to this needy but socially stigmatized group and the justification for allocating scarce resources for these types of services causes intense debate in many countries. In all these countries, criminal justice systems bear a heavy burden in responding to drug problems with extensive use of police time and court time and high rates of imprisonment of the addict population. All of the countries in the region have high imprisonment rates for drug addicts.

Despite limited resources, many countries invest heavily in the management of their drug dependent populations. China has developed an institutional reform program where users are sent after a second relapse into drug use. Similarly, Malaysia makes use of long term institutional correctional methods. In Malaysia there are 27 rehabilitation centers which offer at least two year residential rehabilitation programs.

Thailand has changed its legislation to enable it to deliver maintenance treatment under particular conditions. Overall it is noted that there is a major resistance to the notion of using an agonist substitution drug in the management of opioid dependence.

Practitioners in the differing countries were of the view that due cultural sensitivity was required in each country to the varying views on the management of opioid dependence with maintenance pharmacotherapy. Many thought that additional resources would be required to develop such services. Many also noted that there was a readiness for change in the light of the reported high relapse rates in cases coming from long-term rehabilitation programs.

The continuing growth in the size and scale of the problem, the growth in HIV seroprevalence among injecting drug users and the availability of new treatment agents made it possible to consider developing this modality of treatment in some countries. Drug treatment professionals are keen to develop protocols for treatment trials that would enable full evaluation of drug substitution treatment within the Asian cultural setting. Such an approach would enable policy makers and planners to evaluate the viability of these treatments within the specific Asian context.

There was also an issue of long-term affordability that would require continuous review. In China, in Yunnan province there was a project underway to develop a trial with Buprenorphine as a medicine for agonist pharmacotherapy of opioid dependence. Thailand, Malaysia, the Philippines and Indonesia expressed an interest in further information and possible development of appropriate projects. Opposition to developing substitution treatment programs is substantial.

The majority of the public and general professionals are sceptical about the role of substitution treatment. There is a view that such treatments are regarded as being too soft on the addicts and therefore not attractive from the harder perspective of the politician and policy maker. On the other hand, a view is evolving that the countries in the region have invested fairly heavily in the treatment of opioid dependence and the returns on the current treatment strategies have not been high enough or visible enough.

Also the scale and severity of the problem is continuing to grow despite the best efforts of everyone. Currently there is a mood for considering a change in strategy and the adoption of new approaches. The idea that substitution could be integrated with existing treatment approaches in order to improve the overall outcome seems attractive. It is possible that a highly structured program may have high retention rates, high rates of abstinence from other non-prescribed drugs and possibly high rates of social rehabilitation because of staff and patient acceptance of these highly structured programs.

Virtually all countries in the South East Asia and Western Pacific regions have a substantial treatment infrastructure. The treatment services are staffed by trained personnel with a high level of commitment to the delivery of treatment for the drug dependent population. The expansion and diversification of treatment is a real option due to the skills and network of professionals, which have developed in all these countries over the past three decades.

It is regarded as very important to work closely with village elders in order to inform and educate them about developments in treatment approaches and to look at harnessing their support in developing new treatments, if these treatments are going to be acceptable to the community in the future.

All countries have a broader psychosocial component of treatment built into their services at every level and those countries with long-term rehabilitation programs place a major focus on broader psychosocial rehabilitation. The size of the treatment population and the throughput of cases make it difficult in practice to deliver very intensive or comprehensive post detoxification relapse prevention. In the Asian context, the family is a very important part in the overall treatment process and approaches to involving families in the treatment process were given great emphasis by all treatment providers. Naltrexone is used in a number of countries.

A large-scale research study on the role of Naltrexone has been underway in Malaysia but the project is not yet complete. In China, a multi-center study and an open study have supported the role and efficacy of naltrexone. A separate study conducted in Singapore using a double blind design in a prison release cohort also found significantly better retention in the active drug group. Overall policy makers seem to be more inclined to use the antagonist naltrexone as a maintenance agent because of its non-euphoriant properties and non-agonist properties. Increasing use of prescribed medication such as naltrexone may help to further develop the pharmacotherapy of opioid dependence in the region.

The use of herbal medicine in the detoxification and broader treatment process is an important component of treatment in the region. Many countries placed major.emphasis on this type of approach and valued it highly. Some of the herbal preparations came from China but others from elsewhere. This type of treatment was very accessible but in some situations some special preparations were very costly and major claims were made in the media and in public forums over the benefits of these treatments.

There is a need for significant research, both pre-clinical and clinical in this area to evaluate the efficacy of specified preparations. Such an approach might identify important new pharmacotherapy agents that may contribute significantly to the field of medicine. Overall there is a tension between the promotion of evidence based medical practice and the use of traditional herbal treatments. However, such tensions could be overcome through good research and evaluation that may help to firmly locate herbal treatments in the overall choices of treatment approaches.

Primary care is a very important part of the health care system in all countries. The primary care and community health teams are often key contacts and provide a broad range of intervention to promote health in the community. They are very important for any broad access strategy and are often the workers who have the best picture of what is happening in the community. It has been reported that the level of involvement of primary care in many countries is limited.

In Thailand the community workers and village health volunteers have an important role in working with the hill tribes and the same situation occurs in Laos. In Laos the view was that major health problems contributed to the use of and dependence on opium and that a lack of basic health services was a major reason for opioid dependence in the community. Hopefully, plans in place for the provision and improvement of primary health care systems will play an important role in the prevention of further opium addiction and relapse. Community based primary health care (PHC) support is being implemented. Village Health Volunteers (VHV) have been established and supported in order to improve the health situation. Village health volunteers are improving health related developments and supporting a health prevention strategy designed to improve the effectiveness, relevancy and accessibility of health information and education at village level. The aim is to develop a reduction in demand component with community involvement in order to increase community awareness of the problem of drug addiction.

In Malaysia and in Myanmar the treatment services were based in specialist centers and did not involve primary care. It is reported that a significant amount of monitoring occurs and many countries have central registers where all new treatment episodes are registered. In China, Myanmar, Malaysia, and the Philippines, the police manage this function. However, it is not clear if this creates problems of confidentiality and whether drug users feel able to access services safely.

Although there is a considerable amount of research underway in the region, there is also a need for major research activity. The consensus is that a range of epidemiological studies is needed which could provide a more detailed picture of current and evolving trends in drug problems that will assist in shaping a response. There is considerable opportunity for regional cooperation in studies and regional sharing of skills and cooperation around joint projects.

There is a desire in a number of countries to take part in pharmacotherapy trials of methadone, buprenorphine and naltrexone. A study is underway comparing tincture of opium to methadone and further work in this area is considered to be important and timely. Given the rapid spread of HIV in the region, it is critical that urgent studies are conducted to enable the mobilization of broader prevention strategies that would result in containment of the current spread. In addition, the studies of AIDS vaccines should include a subgroup of injecting drug users, such as is happening in Thailand.

A range of other studies is either underway or at the planning stage on aspects of other drug dependent problems, such as Amphetamine Type Stimulant use and its related psychiatric complications. There are also studies on cannabis, tobacco and alcohol related problems. There is an interest in all countries being involved in multi-center studies and there is an opportunity to conduct short term, high impact, treatment evaluation studies across a number of countries which would assist policy development.

Reports from most countries are that a significant amount of training is underway for generic professionals and for community health workers. However, there is still a major gap in training and there is a need for a far more comprehensive approach to the development of training if the capacity and skill within this field is to be adequately developed over the coming decade.

There is a need to extend basic training but there is also a need for senior training in specialist areas of treatment and research. It is thought that a regional network with a good communication infrastructure could make a contribution to the development of a robust training infrastructure and network within the individual countries. Overall, the challenge of improving training centred on the importance of having adequate resources but also having the manpower and development within a field of work that was attractive to be in and that would attract capable and competent staff who are self-motivated and self-directed.

It was also made clear that a considerable bank of training material exists that was not easy to access and any process that improved access to existing material would be very helpful. Training programmes need to be established with long-term objectives, and with appropriate qualifications and career developments linked in, if they are going to be sustainable and have any impact. There is a strong need to establish a regional treatment and research network that will assist in facilitating communication between research and treatment centres and between countries.

Methadone maintenance treatment is the major treatment modality for opioid dependence in Australia. Therapeutic communities and other drug-free approaches are also available but attract and retain only a small proportion of opiate dependent people. Naltrexone maintenance treatment has become available relatively recently.

Historically most treatment services have been provided by the government, with the exception of therapeutic communities and other drug-free treatments which have tended to be the domain of non-government organizations. This situation is changing, with considerable effort being directed towards encouraging greater involvement of the private sector, particularly general medical practitioners.

Number of persons receiving treatment for opioid dependence. There is a continuing trend of increasing demand for treatment. It is thought that less than 50% of dependent opiate users are currently in treatment. Nationally around 30,000 are currently receiving methadone maintenance treatment. This represents around three-quarters of all those in treatment. The number of people receiving methadone maintenance treatment has been increasing by around 10% per annum for the past decade.

Naltrexone is available for relapse prevention treatment but there are no data on the number of opiate users receiving this treatment. Buprenorphine has recently been registered in Australia but is not yet generally available. However, it is considered likely to become central to treatment options over the next five to ten years. Levo-alpha-acetyl-methadol (LAAM) and slow release morphine are under active investigation in Australia as alternative substitution approaches, but it will be some years before they are likely to become generally available.

Naltrexone became generally available over the last two years while buprenorphine was registered for the treatment of opioid dependence at the end of 2000. Withdrawal treatments for opioid dependence rely on clonidine and symptomatic medications. Methadone is not generally used in Australia as a withdrawal treatment. Buprenorphine is considered to have potential as a withdrawal treatment.

Methadone is a restricted drug. This means that it can only be prescribed and dispensed by approved providers and all patients receiving methadone maintenance treatment are registered with State and Territory health authorities. Arrangements for buprenorphine are still being finalized, but similar restrictions are expected to apply. Naltrexone is more generally available, being listed as a schedule 4 drug. This means that it can be prescribed by any medical practitioner, and dispensed by any pharmacy.

The delivery of effective pharmacotherapy is multidisciplinary, entailing medical practitioners, nurses, pharmacists and counsellors. Most methadone maintenance treatments involve primary health care providers and considerable effort is being expended nationally to maintain this trend. The remainder continue to be treated at clinics or practices with a focus on drug and alcohol issues.

The majority of methadone clients now receive their medication from a community pharmacy. Currently underway is a co-ordinated process of evaluation of pharmacotherapies for opioid dependence. This work will combine the outcomes of recent clinical research in Australia and is expected to provide guidance for future service development. There is also a three state treatment outcome study being undertaken.

Community concern about opioid dependence continues to be high, but understanding of the nature of dependence remains limited. The expressed community view continues to be that treatment should be directed first and foremost to the quick achievement of abstinence. In general the community has little understanding of heroin dependence, reflecting the fact that.most of the community are aware of heroin users primarily through exposure to drug-related criminal activity. This is in turn reflected in community resistance to treatment services, and particularly to methadone dispensing being located in town centers, and to continual questioning of the effectiveness of methadone treatment.

Politicians are of course sensitive to community pressure with the result that there is also a degree of political resistance to expansion of substitution treatments, and a preference for abstinence-based treatments. The public health system in Australia is currently under considerable resource pressure and this situation is likely to continue. Public hospital services are particularly affected.

In China, throughout the 1980s, drug abuse was considered to be at the initial or sporadic stage. The majority of drug-smuggling incidents involved opium only, with heroin accounting for a very small proportion, and drug consumption was limited to border areas in the southwest and rural areas in the northwest of China. Most of the abusers were elderly people. In the 1990's, drug-related crimes became rampant and drug abuse spread quickly. China faced greater challenges than ever before in combating drug-related crimes and preventing drug abuse.

There is no methadone maintenance program available in China. Short-term detoxification programs and antagonist (naltrexone) treatment programs are available and therapeutic community programs also take place. Methadone is widely used as a substitution agent in China, but only the short-term detoxification program is approved by the authorities. The mean duration of methadone treatment is 7 to 20 days. It is reported that success rates of completed detoxification were about 70% to 80%.

The use of non-opiate agents (e.g. Clonidine) in the detoxification of opiate addiction was first studied by Jiang Zuoning and his colleagues in a controlled clinical study. 200 heroin addicts were enrolled. The results showed that the withdrawal scores of both clonidine and methadone groups were sharply decreased daily, suggesting the anti-opiate efficacy be similar. The results also showed that there was a higher incidence of postural hypotension in the clonidine group and drug-seeking behaviours in the methadone group.

The advantages of clonidine are that it is non euphoria provoking and non-addictive, which prevents it becoming a source of illegal sale and.abuse. Other researchers also found that clonidine was effective in suppressing the withdrawal symptoms in different grades. In the meantime, Wang Xiaoping et al, also reported their clinical experience of clonidine in the treatment of opiate addiction, suggesting it was safer and better than subhebernation therapy with chlorpromazine and pethidine. Lofexidine, a clonidine analogue, has also been used to relieve the withdrawal symptoms of opioid dependence since 1998.

Compared with clonidine, lofexidine has similar efficacy and onset in suppressing opiate withdrawal symptoms. It was found that lofexidine had a similar side effects profile, with the exception of hypotensive effects, which was significantly less severe than those on clonidine, especially during the first four days. The study suggested that lofexidine is safer, more desirable, and more suitable for outpatient detoxification of opiate addiction.

Buprenorphine (Bup) is usually categorized into the mixed agonist-antagonist class of opioids. In recent years, its efficacy in suppressing opiate withdrawal syndrome has been well recognized. Buprenorphine is considered a promising agent in the treatment of opioid dependence by many authors. Since its launch on the market, almost a dozen trials on detoxification of heroin abusers with buprenorphine have been conducted in many parts of China, (most guided by the National Institute on Drug Dependence in Beijing). The results are promising.

Many clinicians prefer Buprenorphine to methadone or clonidine both in compulsory and non-compulsory settings. Although influenced by some foreign research, Chinese investigators have carried out their own researches. For example, most Chinese studies are for two weeks instead of the recommended two to seventeen weeks, and the defined daily dose is also lower than that recommended by NIDA. These considerations may be based on the fact that the majority of Chinese drug abusers have a relatively short history of drug use and also a different body composition.

The detox programs with Buprenorphine are more diversified, including a 'Buprenorphine alone program ' and a 'Buprenorphine combined with other agents' program. As all the detoxification programs in China are short-termed, most of them are based on similar dose schedules. The initial dose is individualized, based on the severity of opiate withdrawal syndrome, history of drug use and physiological conditions; then gradually reduced daily until discontinuation in 1 to 2 weeks.

Some empirical observations in non-compulsory inpatient settings showed that more than 80% of the addicts finished the 7 to 12 -day treatment, and fewer side effects were observed than in the clonidine treated population, suggesting its high tolerability. In fact, some addicts preferred this program when several programs were offered to them. However, some Buprenorphine abuse was observed by clinicians.

Traditional Chinese medicine (TCM) has its own theory and practice about opiate addiction. From 1840 to 1952, many addicts received TCM treatment and completed detoxification successfully. During these years, some research units and pharmaceutical factories continued their efforts.

Naltrexone is an opiate antagonist. A multiple-center study that included a double-blind and an open study among 302 heroin addicts, suggested its efficacy in relapse-prevention of heroin addicts. The follow-up study was conducted in 7 treatment centers in China. The study period was six months. Naltrexone was given 50mg/d in the double-blind study and the open study.

The non-euphoric effects reported in both naltrexone and placebo groups were 68.18% and 33.3% respectively. The rate of morphine positive urine tests was 24.38% in the naltrexone group with 40.48% in the placebo group. The adverse drug effects included sleep disturbances, lack of appetite, weakness, diarrhea, anxiety, stomach-ache, aching in bones and muscle, dry mouth, headache, irritability, cold flash, nervousness, nausea and vomiting, dizziness, constipation and skin rash.

Some of the effects could be attributed to symptoms and signs of precipitated abstinence in patients with residual dependence. The results suggested that naltrexone be an adjunct medication in the relapse-prevention of heroin dependents. The authors concluded that the adverse drug effects were very slight, and therefore suitable for maintenance treatment.

According to Chinese law, addicts with two or more relapses will be sent to the rehabilitation labour institutions run by the Departments of Justice. The average stay is about two years and strict regulation makes it possible to stay drug-free for a relatively long time. In the meantime, there are many educational, training and therapeutic programs adapted for the residents. It is estimated that the abstinence rate three years after discharge is 15%.

The clinical trials of multi-centers within the country are taken up in the Department of Clinical Pharmacology in order to assess addictive patients response to anti-morphine dependence agents, including Chinese traditional medicine, Alpha-2 receptor antagonists (e.g. clonidine, lofexidine), μ-receptor antagonist (e.g. naloxone, naltrexone) and the others. Information about drug abuse problems in our country is provided for the Department of Chinese Government by the Department of Drug Epidemiology. Long-term follow-up and surveillance of national drug abuse has been carried out. We have acquired some important material from high-risk regions of drug abuse using epidemiological methods such as demographic and national distributions; proportion of positive HIV; and hepatitis and other physical diseases in drug abusers. A pilot study of National Epidemiology on Substance Dependence is being prepared.

The Chinese Journal of Drug Dependence is edited by the Department of Information on Drug Dependence. We have sponsored and organized many educational programs on substance abuse in the community, in primary schools and high schools and in colleges and universities. Training programs on the prevention and treatment of drug abusers, the management and control of illegal drugs for clinical doctors, government officers and social workers are run by this department. Education on drug abuse is very important in order to protect adolescents and young persons from illegal substances.

Relapse rates are high which has already attracted the attention of both the government and the community. More effort and general interest is being put into drug prevention now. However, although more addicts have the motivation to withdraw from drug abuse, the relapse rate and associated economic problems are puzzling. After care is not available in most communities.

In Hongkong, the great majority of the local population is of Chinese descent. Among foreign residents, Philippine passport holders rank first with 495,200 residents, mostly domestic helpers. Second are Indonesians with 53,400 residents with a similar background. These are followed by Americans, Canadians, Thais, British, Indians, Australians, Japanese and others who are mostly business people or official representatives. The median age of the population is 36.6 with life expectancy at 77.2 years for males and 82.4 for females.

The crude birth rate is 8.0 per 1,000 and the death rate is 4.9 per 1,000. The average wages of all selected industries is HK$ 11,306 p.m. ccount. Since 1998 the unemployment rate has hovered at about 4% to 5%. Due to scarsity of land and relatively high wages, most locally owned industrial production and assembly line industries have relocated northward across the border in the past two or three decades. Hong Kong SAR however, remains one of the financial and communications centres of Asia, having survived the Asian economic crises in the closing years of the 20th century.

Hong Kong SAR also looks forward to a faster recovery than other Asian countries on account of the impending entry of China to the World Trade Organization and the hosting of the 2008 Olympic games in Beijing. The combined effects of these historic events should stimulate tourism related industries as well as international and inter-regional investments on an unprecedented scale.

Nevertheless its continued use persisted underground with the 'protection' of some corrupt law enforcers and part openly in the small walled city of Kowloon, which was supposedly ruled by a Chinese magistrate to administrate Ching Dynasty Civil Laws. He abandoned his enclave in the late 18th century to the control of the Triad Societies. Following the establishment of the Peoples.Republic of China in 1950 and its ironfisted closed door rule on the mainland, opiate use was suppressed forcefully and practically eliminated for a quarter of century, until China's south-western border with the Asian Golden Triangle was reopened for trade in the late 1970s and early '80s.

In fact the land route for opiate smuggling from Northern Myanmar through south-west Yunnan Province via Guangxi and Guangdong Provinces to Hong Kong has, since the 1990s replaced the traditional sea route via Thailand as the leading source of narcotics supply for the lucrative market in Hong Kong SAR up until today.

In post World War II Hong Kong, heroin use rose steadily to replace opium smoking, and intravenous injection increased steadily to overtake the method of smoking through cigarettes, nicknamed the 'firing of anti-aircraft guns', and of fume inhalation, nicknamed 'dragon chasing'. With rapid industrialization and immigration from the mainland, the population grew rapidly from 600,000 at the end of World War II to 3,000,000 by the mid 1950s. The spread of opiate use among immigrants, workers and young people accelerated alarmingly.

In 1958, the Prisons Department (of that time), reported that among 18,410 persons imprisoned that year, 11,863 (64.4%) were narcotic dependents. A White Paper by the Colonial Government in 1959 estimated a total number of 150,000 addicts. In 1973, the newly empowered Action Committee Against Narcotics (ACAN) decided to establish a Central Registry of Drug Abuse (CRDA) to better assess the incidence and prevalence rates of narcotic abuse, but its first report was not published until 1976, following belated computerization of its data processing system. A more realistic estimate of some 50,000 drug abusers out of the four million population was then suggested.

The great majority of these were under-educated male adults, living in public housing, with rather low incomes, mostly engaged in petty crime including theft, prostitution/pimping, illicit gambling and trading or in possession of narcotic drugs. The contribution to public health by a wide network of methadone clinics was demonstrated when tetanus was first diagnosed in 1993 among IDUs maintained on methadone. All 21 clinics in Hong Kong, Kowloon and the New Territories were promptly converted into prevention centres and thousands of IDUs received immunization and education against tetanus in the subsequent weeks. A potential epidemic was thus nipped in the bud.

The main types of treatment programmes for drug dependence include a compulsory placement programme operated by the Correctional Services Department (CSD), a voluntary out-patient methadone programme provided by the Department of Health, and voluntary residential treatment programmes run by the Caritas-Hong Kong, SARDA and other non-governmental organizations (NGOs), including nine Christian spiritual rehabilitation agencies, once known as 'Non-Medical Treatment Centres' because they practiced 'cold turkey withdrawal'. In recent years, most of them have made arrangements for their patients who need medication to be placed elsewhere first. The CSD runs two drug addiction treatment centres.

The voluntary methadone treatment programme operated by the Department of Health includes both maintenance and detoxification options for outpatients. Under the more popular maintenance scheme, patients are provided with an appropriate dose of methadone each day to block their craving for heroin. The much smaller detoxification program aims to wean patients off drugs by gradually reducing their daily dosage of methadone until they are completely drug-free or referred to residential care. Social counselling and public health education are provided to all patients, and drug dependent persons seeking help are able to select any type of treatment. There are 21 methadone clinics at present attended by an average of about 7,000 patients daily. On the other hand, all the other combined voluntary treatment programmes cater for five or six hundred drug-dependent persons at any one time and re-integrate them into the society.

The Department of Health provides subvention to Caritas to operate a youth treatment centre for young men and to SARDA for adult men and women, and male and female teenagers separately in four residential treatment centres with a total capacity of 450 beds.Since 1963, SARDA has provided medical detoxification and psychosocial rehabilitation services to over 60,000 male and 2,500 female cases including re-admissions. Presently about

2,000 voluntary patients per annum are admitted to its residential rehabilitation programme. All programme leavers are encouraged to join the Pui Hong Self-Help Association for continuing mutual support.

The Social Welfare Department (SWD) also provides subvention to four non-government organizations, which provide voluntary long-term residential treatment programmes emphasizing a Christian spiritual approach. They are the Barnabas Charitable Service Association, Ling Oi Youth Centre of the Finnish Missionary Society, Operation Dawn and Christian New Being Fellowship, which in total provide 309 places for mainly narcotic dependents. The length and content of the programmes vary with the four organisations, which also provide various aftercare services.

For the treatment of psychotropic substance abusers, subvented counselling services are provided by PS33 of the Hong Kong Christian Service, Cheer Lutheran Centre of Hong Kong Lutheran Social Service and the Caritas HUGS Centre. Two teams of specially trained social workers have been set up under the Against Substance Abuse Scheme of the SWD to help youth at risk who occasionally misuse drugs. There are also six Substance Abuse Clinics established by the Hospital Authority to provide medical services primarily to psychotropic substance abusers. However, they also support the above-mentioned NGOs who do not have their own medical facility for treating withdrawal symptoms or detoxification complications.

In reality many psychotropic abusers may progress into narcotic use and opiate dependents may also abuse a variety of other drugs intermittently such as alcohol, tranquilizers, hypnotics and anaesthetics, especially when the dosage of methadone maintenance appears to be inadequate to some individuals. The colloquial description of such multiple drug abuse is 'double or triple fried dishes'. Although all treatment and rehabilitation agencies report to CRDA about their newly admitted cases, they do not always report premature discharges or relapses under aftercare.

Hence CRDA could not at present fulfill one of its original objectives for programme evaluation.The so-called 'success rates'"claimed by individual centres do not follow any standard criteria of measurement at present and if relapsed cases are counted at the close of aftercare service, they usually do not specify any length of prior abstinence under follow-up.

Today, Indonesia has become a producer and exporter of drugs. In the year 2000 the total population of Indonesia reached more than 210 million people, of which the youth proportion is about 40 %. As in other countries, young people between the ages of 15 and 25 years are the most vulnerable to drug abuse. This is due to the psychological and behavioral attitudes of adolescents and their search for an identity.

Indonesia has had a drug problem for quite a long time. It is estimated that drugs were introduced at the time of Chinese immigrant arrivals. At first, drugs were taken habitually especially amongst fishermen in order to keep up their endurance. This situation changed during the Dutch colonial regime which benefited from the habit when they decided to expand their plantations to other islands outside Java, where opium was then legally sold and distributed amongst the Chinese community. Also amongst certain tribes opium was used as a local custom, rather like alcoholic drink is consumed at special events or ceremonies.

Since the first morphine addict was treated in one of the private mental hospitals in Jakarta in 1969, drug abuse in Indonesia had been relatively low and consistent involving sleeping pills, marijuana, alcohol, and small amounts of morphine, heroin and amphetamines. But from 1990 a dramatic change took place in the trend of drug abuse in Indonesia. Beginning with stimulant drugs such as ecstasy, the trend later developed into the use of 'putauw', (the street name for heroin) as the most popular drug amongst young adults. These are indications of the increasing problem in recent years :

Many ways of combating drug abuse have been attempted in Indonesia. The first step for treatment, as well as rehabilitation is to know or identify the basic substance abuse because of the problems of social stigma. The next step is the identification of health and psycho-social problems that usually go along with the main problem. The role of counselling is needed to change behaviour such as motivating the patients to stop abusing drugs by giving them information about the risks of drug abuse and the benefits of addiction treatment. Abusers who have been motivated towards a cure, have to be referred to the rehabilitation program as soon as possible.

A well known form of detoxification used is opioid detoxification, in which the abuser is given opiate substitution and symptomatic pharmacotherapy, e.g. Codeine, which is easy to obtain in addition to Chinese/ Korean Herbal therapy with oral pills (traditional herbs), as an alternative pharmacotherapy. The Indonesian government does not support the use of Methadone as a substitute for heroin addiction treatment. However, many individual experts consider that Methadone is good enough for that purpose. On the other hand, Clonidine that does not contain opioid is rarely used as a substitute substance because of its side effects. With regard to the use of levo-alpha-acetyl-methadol (LAAM) and Buprenorphine, it is regretted that those substances are not yet available in Indonesia.

In northern Laos, opium is commonly used as a painkiller and opium addiction is a real problem among some of the ethnic minority groups in this region. The use of opium as a painkiller over a fairly long period of time was given as the main reason for addiction. There were reports of heroin availability and use. Abuse of psychotropic substances (e.g. ATS) does not appear to be common yet. However, it is feared this could be the next form of drug of abuse by current day glue sniffing methods.

A tincture of opium detoxification is the major detoxification modality for opioid dependence in Laos. To date, there are many verbal and mixed reports of attempts at various treatment activities in the different provinces and districts and different experiences by different ethnic groups and communities. These include social mobilization to provide education about the dangerous effects of drug use, awareness campaigns, and the use of herbal/ traditional medicines for detoxification, detoxification carried out by private medical practitioners and resettlement programs.

Basically, most treatment services have been provided by the UNDCP and NGO's funding. Drug control projects in Laos include a social development component and the establishment of a primary health care system. Although these projects are better known as opium reduction projects, they are in fact aimed at both supply and demand reduction. A number of the activities included the treatment and rehabilitation component but there is a need to develop sustainable treatment and rehabilitation capacities at both the levels of design strategy and the levels of operation.

Drug addiction has increased tremendously in Malaysia since the 1970's. Over these years, heroin abuse has been on the increase. However, there was a decline in heroin abuse in the year 2000, from 17,429 in 1999 compared to 13,605 in 2000. Most heroin users also use other drugs. The combination of morphine, cannabis cough mixtures, amphetamine-type stimulants (ATS) and opium causes substantial concern as these drug combinations increase the risk of overdose.

Malaysia has seen an increasing trend among IDU's causing the spread of HIV infection. As of 2001 the number of HIV cases detected included 658,93 suffering from chronic illnesses, and 28 cases with psychiatric related disorders. The policy in Malaysia, is that once a drug addict has been identified as having full-blown HIV infection, he/she will be discharged from the drug rehabilitation center. The National Drug Information System (NADI) which is attached to the National Drugs Agency does not keep reports of overdose cases. This is because almost all of them die on the streets and are immediately

Some of the approaches include the Therapeutic Community (TC) modality, Multi-Disciplinary modality (Psychosocial), Religious Oriented modality and Work Therapy modality. There are 27 government-managed centers that can cater for 12,000 addicts at any one time. Treatment and rehabilitation in government managed centers are free of charge. In year 2000, 14,094 addicts were rehabilitated in these 27.centers. There are also 56 registered NGO managed drug rehabilitation centers.

However, these NGO centers treat very small numbers of addicts and they charge for treatment and rehabilitation.

The Government launched a pilot project using naltrexone as an adjunct drug for rehabilitation. However, the decision to continue with this project will be dependent on the result of the pilot project. Naltrexone and clonidine have already been used in the treatment of addicts in a number of Government managed hospitals. The law provides for two modalities in treatment and rehabilitation. Addicts can either be sent to rehabilitation centers for institutional rehabilitation or to the community for community treatment and rehabilitation.

Methadone is not used in Malaysia as a treatment method or in maintenance treatment. Naltrexone and clonidine are restricted drugs. These drugs can only be prescribed by medical practitioners and dispensed by pharmacies from General Hospitals. All these patients are registered with the health authorities. Most of the dispensing and supervision of medication is done by the hospital sectors. The majority of cases now also receive their medication from private pharmacies.

Before 1970, opium users were scattered among the poppy cultivation areas of hilly regions. They consisted of just the older physical workers and used opium as a relaxant, as a medicine for self-treatment of coughs and diarrhoea and for traditional and cultural usage. The average age of initiation was 30 years and the mean age was found to be 41 years and they were from below average social classes. Most of them were married males living with their families. They used a low dosage of opium with low tolerance, which was cheap and used either the smoking or ingestion route with few problems.

Methadone was also used in the mid 1970s but was omitted after a comparative study made between the 'cold turkey' method, the substituting symptomatic method and methadone detoxification. It was found that the 'cold turkey' method was inhumane. The patients suffered a lot and became less confident in the treatment service. Methadone was satisfactory, but in comparison with Tincture of Opium, was found to be less effective. Tincture of Opium with analgesic and chlorpromazine tablets used in gradual reduction methods over a period of 10 to 14 days was also found to be satisfactory in suppressing withdrawal syndromes.

Methadone was very expensive and had to be imported and therefore this therapy was left out. As Tincture of Opium (T.0) is a cheap local product (produced by the Myanmar Pharmaceutical Industry) and equally effective compared to Methadone, it was introduced to all drug treatment centers in the country. Inpatient services were given preference because of the relapse problems of outpatients and their.likelihood of arrest by law enforcement officers operating the Drug Law. The DTCs usually give detoxification programs to addicts rather than put them on maintenance programs.

Under the direction of the Ministry of Health, drug education is provided as a component of health education in all middle and high schools run by the Department of Basic Education. IEC activities are being carried out at all 30 DTCs, in the country and hospitals in border areas. In 1999, 5 research works were carried out with assistance from WHO. Psychiatrists stationed at major DTCs in States and Divisions conducted these projects.

Mental health is generally a specialized service provided only in the national institution in Manila and in some regions. Recently a move was made to integrate it into the tertiary general hospitals that are national facilities and enjoy comparatively better resource allocations than the devolved hospitals government run, 534 were devolved and the 53 that consisted of medical centers, special and regional hospitals were retained.

A physician, nurse, midwife, sanitary inspector, dentist and a medical technologist man a typical health center. The latter two are each responsible for two or three municipalities. A strengthened referral system among the facilities ensures a smooth and uninterrupted delivery of services. In 2001, the health sector reform agenda started to be implemented and is ongoing. Community based organizations have been established as initiated by the health sector, leading to a more integrated and co-ordinated approach to health and overall development, In Manila, Alcoholics Anonymous (AA) and Narcotics Anonymous meetings are regularly held in selected localities.

There is no reported admission of opioid dependence in the national mental institutions and regional psychiatric hospitals. An interview of a key informant at Makati Medical Centre (MMC), a private medical center catering for affluent families, revealed that 5 to 8 opioid dependent patients have been admitted in the past two years. These patients belong to the uppermost economic bracket in the Philippines and some were foreigners who had decided to be admitted to the MMC. In 1998, heroin was reported to be a part of seized drugs in police campaigns against illicit trafficking. From 1999 to the present, no heroin seizures have been reported.

For opiate withdrawal, morphine is given intramuscularly and clonidine orally to titrate the withdrawal symptoms. For patients taking opiates with benzodiazepines, withdrawal from benzodiazepines is prioritized. No long term follow-up is observed upon discharge. Patients come for admission when their supply is held up or has been consumed, hence causing the withdrawals. It is observed that the same patients come for admission at least once a year. Currently, the government has no treatment facility for opioid dependence. Since opiate dependents are from the higher social economic bracket, they can afford to attend private medical centers.

Drug abuse treatment methods in Thailand are divided into three systems:

Voluntary System

This gives an opportunity for drug addicts to voluntarily decide to get treatment in medical centers in both the public and private sectors. The Ministry of Public Health has issued a Public Health Regulation for the voluntary treatment of substance dependence. The Regulation defines how management and treatment services operate. The treatment service is under licensing control and includes four stages.

1. Pre-admission within 7 days
2. detoxification within 45 days
3. rehabilitation within 180 days
4. after care within 1 year.

In the area drug abuse of treatments, in order to respond to the increase in the drug abuse problem, there are at present 710 treatment centers. 627 are run by government agencies and 83 are run by the private sector.

2. *Correctional system*

The system is to treat drug addicts who have been found guilty of crimes and imprisoned. The drug addicts are required to get treatment by law. The system is operated under the Ministry of the Interior.

3. *Compulsory system*

It is legally enforced that drug addicts get treatment under the Drug Addict rehabilitation Act, B.E. 2534. This means that suspects in drug cases are required to have their urine tested and to get treatment by the rehabilitation programs within a specific period. At present, this system is not yet implemented. The system will operate under the jurisdiction of the Ministry of Justice. Admission to the system is strictly under court judgement. Methadone detoxification treatment is the major treatment for opioid dependence in Thailand. In response to the IVDU problems, the Department of Medical Services was forced to review and amend the Narcotics Law B.E. 2522, by supporting long term Methadone Treatment. This began in September, 2000.

Methadone detoxification treatment is the major treatment for opioid dependence in Thailand. Therapeutic communities and other drug free approaches are also available but attract and retain only a small proportion of opiate dependent people. Naltrexone treatment has become available recently. It was registered and approved by Thailand FDA in 1997.

It was indicated as a treatment of alcohol dependence. It is very expensive but is considered of use in some groups of patients especially in the private sector.

Buprenorphine has been registered for the relief of moderate and severe pain but its use for the treatment of opioid dependence is not currently registered.

As indicated above methadone detoxification remains dominant. Long term methadone treatment or methadone maintenance has just been approved and amended by The Narcotics Act B.E.2522, so it will become generally available. Withdrawal treatment for opioid dependence relies on clonidine and symptomatic medications. Naltrexone and Buprenorphine is not generally in use in Thailand as a withdrawal treatment..Legislation and control mechanisms Methadone is restricted. It is listed as a schedule 2 in the Narcotics Act B.E. 2522. It can only be prescribed and dispensed by physicians, and all patients receiving methadone maintenance are registered with drug dependence treatment clinics and reports are sent to the Narcotics Control Division FDA.

Buprenorphine is listed as schedule 3 in the Psychotropic Substance Act B.E. 2518. It is restricted to be prescribed by physicians or dispensed by any pharmacist with the physician's prescription. Naltrexone is more generally available, being listed as a specially controlled drug with a safety -monitoring program. This means that it is able to be prescribed by physicians in all government sectors and private sectors which are drug dependence treatment clinics according to the Narcotics Act B.E. 2522 and some private sectors that treat alcoholic dependence. The delivery of effective pharmacotherapy is multidisciplinary through medical practitioners, nurses and pharmacists.

The majority of methadone clients now receive their medication from a community pharmacy by a physician's prescription. There is a trend of increasing involvement of community pharmacies for dispensing and supervising the administration of methadone. Some clients obtain methadone from nurses or medical practitioners in methadone clinics.

Personal Construct Theory

Personal construct theory is a notion about how man may launch out from a position of admitted ignorance, and how he may aspire from one day to the next to transcend his own dogmatisms. It is, then, a theory of man's personal inquiry-a psychology of human quest. It does not say what has been or will be found, but proposes rather how we might go about looking for it. Like other theories, the psychology of personal constructs is the implementation of a philosophical assumption. In this case the assumption is that whatever nature may be, or howsoever the quest for truth will turn out in the end, the events we face today are subject to as great a variety of construction as our wits will enable us to contrive.

This philosophical position we have called constructive alternativism, and its implications, keep cropping up in the psychology of personal constructs. It can be contrasted with the prevalent epistemological assumption of accumulative fragmentalism, which is that truth is collected piece by piece. While constructive alternativism does not argue against the collection of information, neither does it measure truth by the size of the collection. Indeed it leads one to regard a large accumulation of facts as an open invitation to some farreaching reconstruction which will reduce them to a mass of trivialities.

A person who spends a great deal of his time hoarding facts is not likely to be happy at the prospect of seeing them converted into rubbish. He is more likely to want them bound and preserved, a memorial to his personal achievement. A scientist, for example, who thinks this way, and especially a psychologist who does so, depends upon his facts to furnish the ultimate proof of his propositions. With these shining nuggets of truth in his grasp it seems unnecessary for him to take responsibility for the conclusions he claims they thrust upon him.

Constructive alternativism stresses the importance of events. But it looks to man to propose what the character of their import shall be. The meaning of an event-that is to say, the meaning we ascribe to it-is anchored in its antecedents and its consequents. Thus meaning displays itself to us mainly in the dimension of time. This is much more than saying that meanings are rehearsals of outcomes, a proposition implicit in behaviouristic theory, or that the ends justify the means-the ethical statement of the same proposition.

Besides including anticipated outcomes, meaning includes also the means by which events are anticipated. This is to suggest that different meanings are in-volved when identical events are correctly anticipated by different sets of inferences. It suggests also the implication of quite different meanings when the basic assumptions are different, even when the chains of inference are otherwise more or less similar.

One of the most exciting aspects of constructive alternativism is its bearing upon the conduct of human inquiry. According to the canons of logic, a statement, if meaningful, is either true or not true. Indeed, the logical positivists have reversed the logic and argued that the criterion for meaningfulness is whether or not a statement can be proved true or not true. This seems to mean that we should not ask a question until we have answered it. But constructive alternativism suggests that the canon itself is not fruitful, or at least that it tends to stultify fruitful endeavour.

Since theories-so far, at least-are devised by men, it seems unreasonable to claim that they are shaped by any process other than a psychological one. A person's processes are psychologically channelized by the ways in which he anticipates events. This is what we have proposed as a fundamental postulate for the psychology of personal constructs. This is a psychological theory. Mostly this is a way of announcing in the basic postulate that we make no commitment to the terms of other disciplines, such as physiology or chemistry. Some have suggested that personal construct theory not be called a psychological theory at all, but a metatheory. There is also the question of whether or not it is a cognitive theory.

Personal construct theory has also been categorized by responsible scholars as an emotional theory, a learning theory, a psychoanalytic theory, a typically American theory, a Marxist theory, a Thomistic theory, a behaviouristic theory, an Apollonian theory, a pragmatistic theory, a reflective theory, and no theory at all. It has also been classified as nonsense, which indeed, by its own admission, it will likely some day turn out to be. In each case there were some convincing arguments offered for the categorization.

The fourth term in the postulate-channelized-was chosen as one less likely than others to imply dynamics. Personal construct theory is elaborated by a string of eleven corollaries which may be loosely inferred from its basic postulate. Beyond these are certain notions of more limited applicability which fall in line with personal construct thinking- notions about such matters as anxiety, guilt, hostility, decision making, creativity, the strategy of psychological research, and other typical concerns of professional psychologists.

Persons differ from each other in their constructions of events. Having assumed that construction is a personal affair, it seems unlikely that any two persons would ever happen to concoct identical systems. Each person characteristically evolves, for his convenience in anticipating events, a construction system embracing ordinal relationships between constructs. If a person is to live actively within his construction system, it must provide him with some clear avenues of inference and movement. There must be ways for him to resolve the more crucial contradictions and conflicts that inevitably arise. This is not to say that all inconsistencies must be resolved at once. Some private paradoxes can be allowed to stand indefinitely, and, in the face of them, one can remain indecisive or can vacillate between alternative expectations of what the future holds in store for him.

A person's construction system is composed of a finite number of dichotomous constructs. But personal construct theory is no more a cognitive theory than it is an affective or a conative one. There are grounds for distinction that operate in one's life that seem to elude verbal expression. A personal construct system can hardly be said to have universal utility. Not everything that happens in the world can be projected upon all the dichotomies that make up a person's outlook.

A person's construction system varies as he successively construes the replications of events. If those constructions are never altered, all that happens during a man's years is a sequence of parallel events having no psychological impact on his life. But if he invests himself-the most intimate event of all-in the enterprise, the outcome, to the extent that it differs from his expectation or enlarges upon it, dislodges the man's construction of himself. In recognizing the inconsistency between his anticipation and the outcome, he concedes a discrepancy between what he was and what he is. A succession of such investments and dislodgements constitutes the human experience.

Confirmation may lead to reconstruing quite as much as disconfirmation-perhaps even more. A confirmation gives one an anchorage in some area of his life, leaving him free to set afoot adventuresome explorations nearby, as, for example, in the case of a child whose security at home emboldens him to be the first to explore what lies in the neighbour's yard. The unit of experience is, therefore, a cycle embracing five phases: anticipation, investment, encounter, confirmation or disconformation, and constructive revision.

Certainly in personal construct theory's line of reasoning experience is not composed of encounters alone. The variation in a person's construction system is limited by the permeability of the constructs within whose ranges of convenience the variants lie.While the Experience Corollary suggests that a man can revise his constructions on the basis of events and his invested anticipations of them, there are limitations that must be taken into account. He must have a construct system which is sufficiently open to novel events to let him know when he has encountered them, else the experience cycle will fail to function in its terminal phases. He must have a system which also will admit the revised construct that emerges at the end of the cycle. If the revised construct is left to stand as an isolated axis of reference, it will be difficult for him to chart any coordinated course of action that takes account of it; he therefore can do little with respect to it except vacillate.

Perhaps it is clear from these remarks that what is meant by permeability is not a construct's plasticity, or its amenability to change within itself, but its capacity to be used as a referent for novel events and to accept new subordinate constructions within its range of convenience. A notion of God, for example, which includes an unabridged dictionary of all things holy, is likely to be impermeable. Anything new that turns up-such as an unbiblical event or idea-is likely to be excluded from the construct's realm of concern. Unless the novelty can fit elsewhere into some more permeable part of the construct system, it is likely to be ignored.

To the extent that one person employs a construction of experience which is similar to that employed by another, his processes are psychologically similar to those of the other person. On the face of it, this corollary appears to assert pretty much what personal construct theory seems to stand for:The notion that behaviour is governed by constructs. But there is more to it than what such a simplified statement might be taken to imply.

But what thoughtful behaviourists have in mind when they make behaviour the focus of their concern is the logical positivist position that anything that cannot be identified as behaviour is untestable and therefore a scientific distraction. Personal construct theory would lead to be concerned with the whole experiential cycle and the process which it represents, rather than with the behavioural phase only.

This corollary makes it possible to say that two persons who have confronted quite different events, and who might have gone through experiential cycles which actually seem to us to be quite different, might nevertheless end up with similar constructions of their experiences, and, because of that, thereafter pursue psychologically similar processes of further inquiry.

Thus personal construct theory further releases psychology from assumptions about the identity of events and man's dependence on them. It leaves us free to envision man coping with 'familiar' events in new ways and cooperating with other men to produce novelties which make their world a different place to live in. Neither behaviourism nor phenomenology, provides a psychological basis for this kind of forward movement in man.

To the extent that one person construes the construction processes of another, he may play a role in a social process involving the other person. Most psychological theories, both 'mechanistic' ones and 'dynamic' ones, regard the experience of guilt as a derivative of punishment. One feels guilty because he thinks he has made himself eligible for punishment. But suppose one does not see punishment as the appropriate treatment of wrong-doing, only as revenge by injured persons serving simply to make clear that they have been hurt.

From the standpoint of personal construct theory, guilt is the sense of having lost one's core role structure. A core structure is any one that is maintained as a basic referent of life itself.Without it a person has no guidelines for staying alive. To the extent that one's core structure embodies his role also, as we have defined role, he is vulnerable to the experience of guilt. He has only to perceive himself dislodged from such a role to suffer the inner torment most of us know so well.

The important decision cycles and creativity cycles which the theory envisions remain unmentioned until this moment, as does a radically different view of dependency. There are strictly psychological definitions of threat, impulsivity, anxiety, transference, preemption, constellatoriness and propositionality. There is a linguistic system called the language of hypothesis, an ontology exemplified in orchestrated approaches to psychotherapy, and a methodology of psychological research.

Counselling for Women with Breast Cancer

Today, the diversity of the population, each woman will experience a range of practical, psychological and emotional challenges as a result of her diagnosis and treatment. These may include: coping with the shock of diagnosis; treatment side effects, such as nausea, vomiting, fatigue and physical changes in body appearance and functioning. The life of each woman may be further disrupted by changes in role and family functioning, occupational or employment and financial status.

Many women will also have to come to terms with progressive illness and approaching death. The psychological impact of breast cancer and its demands are significant. The experience of breast cancer may continue to have an emotional impact on some women long after their diagnosis. Residual concerns about recurrence and fear of checkups may last for many years after the original diagnosis. The diagnosis of a recurrence is a very stressful time, and up to 50 per cent of women experience psychiatric disorders at this time.

Much can be done to improve a woman's adjustment to the diagnosis and treatment of breast cancer. Each woman will have her own ways of coping which may have helped in the past, and which may include religious faith or specific problem solving techniques. All members of the treatment team may also play a role in strengthening the woman's own resources by providing additional emotional, informational and practical assistance, and appropriately fostering a sense of hope or optimism.

Cumulative evidence now demonstrates that psychological therapies improve emotional adjustment and social functioning, and reduce both treatment and disease-related distress in cancer patients. In Australia, a meta-analysis of 45 randomised controlled trials in cancer patients, those receiving psychological therapies had, on average, a significant improvement of 12 per cent in emotional adjustment, 10 per cent in social functioning, 14 per cent in treatment and disease-related symptoms, and 14 per cent in overall improvement in their quality of life when compared to those not receiving psychological therapies.

A meta-analysis of intervention studies showed that cancer patients receiving psycho-educational or psychosocial interventions had much lower rates of anxiety, depression, mood disturbances, nausea, vomiting and pain, and significantly greater knowledge about disease and treatment, than no intervention controls.Evidence from meta-analyses of randomised controlled trials indicates the efficacy of both supportive and cognitive-behavioural therapies in the treatment of depressive disorders in women with breast cancer, and the efficacy of both individual and group therapies.

A large body of evidence indicates that psychosocial interventions can benefit the emotional adjustment and social functioning of cancer patients. However, there are few guidelines available on providing direct psychosocial interventions and the provision of supportive care for women with breast cancer. The Psychosocial clinical practice guidelines: providing information, support and counselling for women with breast cancer, and their implementation and evaluation strategy, have been developed following the steps and parameters recommended by the NHMRCin response to this need.

Psychosocial Clinical Practice

The objective of the psychosocial clinical practice guidelines is to assist health professionals in achieving the goal of providing an evidence base for all aspects of the clinical care of women with breast cancer, by documenting recommendations derived from the best available evidence on the psychosocial aspects of care. The provision of optimal care is reliant upon effective physical and psychological care. The psychosocial clinical practice guidelines augments the treatment guidelines by providing evidence-based recommendations on:

— the provision of information;

— the integration of quality of life issues into the care of women with breast cancer;

— minimising the social and psychological impact of breast cancer on a woman and her family; and

— strategies for the identification and management of women experiencing significant emotional disturbance.

These guidelines identify fundamental themes in the provision of psychological care and all evidence-based recommendations detailed herein merit attention and action. It is acknowledged however, that local circumstances and the availability of resources may influence the implementation of some recommendations. Indeed, some recommendations may be difficult to implement due to local resource constraints, such as the current availability of psychiatrists, clinical psychologists or specialist breast nurses. Therefore, the guidelines are not rigid procedural paths, they are intended to allow flexibility in their implementation, dependent upon available resources and individual treatment centre characteristics.

These guidelines were developed for use by all members of the diagnostic and treatment team, which may include surgeons, radiation oncologists, medical oncologists, general practitioners, nurses, social workers, psychologists, psychiatrists, physiotherapists and occupational therapists. It is recognised that while some aspects of psychosocial care are common to all the health professionals involved in a woman's treatment and care, different members of the treatment team will be responsible for specific aspects of the psychosocial care of women with breast cancer.

Information about breast cancer and treatment information often has considerable emotional impact on women. If women are confronted with treatment-related information in a distracting environment (eg an open ward) or by professionals who they perceive to be rushed and unsupportive (eg during a ward round), much information can be forgotten, satisfaction compromised and poor adjustment may result.

A woman with breast cancer is likely to be faced with multiple concerns that can vary widely and change across time. They include coping with fears over her health and future, undergoing unpleasant treatments and coping with physical symptoms. They can also include practical concerns such as not being able to do things that are important to her, and the possible impact of her illness on employment and financial stability.

Women often report feelings like 'being in a state of shock', 'feeling out of control' or being angry, fearful or helpless. Grief and loss are often key issues. Breast cancer can be stressful for women of all ages, however younger women are likely to face unique concerns and may be particularly vulnerable. Women may be concerned about the impact of breast cancer on their partner and children including practical issues such as the availability of childcare.

There is evidence that the coping of the woman affects the whole family. The extent to which a woman has support and feels supported, has been identified as an important factor in women's adjustment to breast cancer. Women with poor support are more likely to experience the additional burden of psychological difficulties. Women with breast cancer, provided with an opportunity to explore feelings with a member of the treatment team or counsellor, experienced less psychosocial distress, such as body image concerns and depression, than women not provided with this opportunity.

Randomised controlled trials also demonstrate that women who received supportive care from a specialist breast nurse had lower rates of psychological distress, such as depression and anxiety, and increased levels of knowledge about treatment compared to those who did not receive such care.

Social support can be provided by health care professionals, family and friends, or support services like the Breast Cancer Support Service (BCSS). The BCSS describes its services as practical and emotional support to those diagnosed with breast cancer. This support is offered on a one-to-one basis and is provided by breast cancer survivors who are two years post-treatment and have been trained for this purpose. They are matched to the service recipient by age, treatment type, and other relevant factors. Contact with the BCSS can be arranged through the state and territory cancer organisations; its leaflet, 'The Breast Cancer Support Service-for health professionals' provides a useful outline of its work.

Psychological Care

In addition to the general effects on a woman's emotional well-being, breast cancer places her at risk of developing a number of specific difficulties with a high psychological impact. These include body image and sexuality problems, interpersonal difficulties, and coping with acute and chronic physical symptoms. Most women will experience minor or transient symptoms of anxiety and depression, and a smaller number of women with breast cancer will develop more severe problems, such as clinical depression, and will require specialised treatment.

Although psychological problems, including body image disturbance, depression and anxiety are common in women with breast cancer, they are frequently underrecognised and under-treated. This may be partly because many women are reluctant to mention their distress to their doctor, because they feel that depression or anxiety are signs of personal weakness. Some clinicians are also reluctant to ask about psychological problems because of their belief that depression and anxiety are a 'normal' response to cancer.

Body image

Body image is a component of self-concept and involves the perception and evaluation of one's body, appearance and functioning.Breast cancer, and its treatment, can significantly change the way a woman thinks and feels about her whole body and femininity, her self-esteem and the way she behaves, alone and with others. Early studies indicated that mastectomy scars, prostheses and the development of lymphoedema caused a devastating impact on the lives of almost one in four women with breast cancer.

More recent data indicate that significant problems often continue. Issues associated with appearance (cosmesis), are important factors for many women making treatment decisions and in adjusting to changes during and after treatments such as surgery and chemotherapy. Although it is thought that cosmesis may be particularly important for women under 55 years of age,body image issues should not be discounted in older women. For some women, concerns about body image, fear of deformity and mutilation, and loss of femininity are significant factors in choosing breast conservation, in some cases even against their doctor's advice.

After treatment, it is important to explore sensitively how the woman is coping with her altered appearance. It can be helpful to ask about the degree of distress this is causing, and the extent to which she avoids situations such as catching sight of herself, allowing her partner to see her naked or undressing in public changing rooms. When a woman is worried about the changes to her body, it is important to assess the nature, severity and impact of these concerns.

Support and education from a specialist breast nurse may help with adjustment difficulties but in more severe cases, the woman may be referred to a clinical psychologist or psychiatrist for appropriate interventions such as cognitive behavioural, supportive or crisis therapy. The clinician needs to be aware that a woman may also avoid sight of her altered breast or be disturbed by images of it because of fear of recurrence and fear of the cancer. In either case, it is important that she is offered a referral to a trained specialist who is able to assess these difficulties thoroughly and provide treatment as needed.

During the treatment of women with breast cancer a number of fertility issues may arise, including the selection of appropriate contraception and the potential for loss of fertility. These issues are of concern to many women and their partners. Loss of fertility may be the source of psychological distress. Although there is insufficient evidence to make specific recommendations on the discussion of fertility issues, awareness of fertility issues by clinicians and providing an opportunity for sensitive discussion, may allow women to consider the potential impact of treatment on their fertility.

Interpersonal problems

The impact of breast cancer can place considerable strain on relationships, particularly in cases where difficulties existed before the diagnosis of breast cancer. Poor marital or family functioning may place a women with breast cancer at increased risk of psychological problems.Women may feel reluctant to discuss their interpersonal problems because they feel embarrassed that they are not coping, or because they feel that nothing can be done. There is however, evidence to indicate that appropriate psychological interventions are effective in the management of interpersonal problems.

Women experiencing interpersonal problems may be offered a referral to couple or family counselling. In addition, family members should also be offered the opportunity to discuss concerns with the clinician or be referred to an appropriate counsellor.

Coping with physical symptoms

Women with breast cancer experience a number of illness and treatment-related physical symptoms that may significantly affect their quality of life and increase the risk of developing more serious levels of anxiety and depression. These include nausea and vomiting, acute and chronic pain, fatigue and lymphoedema. Psychological interventions may be helpful to reduce the distress and impairment associated with these symptoms and, in some cases, to reduce the severity of the symptom itself.

Chemotherapy

Despite recent improvements in anti-emetics,

chemotherapy-induced nausea and vomiting continue to cause significant suffering. In some cases, women will develop habitual nausea and vomiting which affects them over and above the direct effects of the chemotherapy. The habitual nausea and vomiting may occur prior to a scheduled administration of chemotherapy or in response to stimuli, such as tastes, smells and locations that have become associated with the chemotherapy.

Women suffering from persistent nausea and vomiting may benefit from psychological interventions, including cognitive-behavioural techniques such as progressive muscle relaxation, guided imagery and systematic desensitisation, supportive interventions and education, all of which have been shown to help.

Pain may arise for a number of reasons in women with breast cancer. Historytaking, examination, and appropriate investigation and treatment of pain are key aspects of clinical care.Pain also has an emotional dimension and for patients with serious illness, the interpretation of the meaning of the pain may influence the way the individual deals with it, as may social, family, personality and cultural factors.

There are a number of psychological approaches, which have been shown to be efficacious in the management of acute and chronic pain in women with breast cancer. These include progressive muscle relaxation, guided imagery and other techniques. In addition, antidepressant medication may be a useful adjunct when treatment with opioid analgesia is required.

There is increasing recognition of the impact of fatigue on a woman's psychological wellbeing during and after treatment for breast cancer. Some studies have reported an association between treatment related fatigue and depressed mood, with both radiotherapy and chemotherapy. Frequent use of quality of life questionnaires that include measures of fatigue, will assist in the understanding of its relationship to psychological morbidity, and its prevalence as a chronic condition persisting beyond treatment cessation.

The precise incidence of lymphoedema is unclear, but is of considerable concern to women who have been treated for breast cancer. Lymphoedema usually occurs between the acute and palliative care phase. The diagnosis of lymphoedema may be a time of considerable stress. In some cases, the woman may avoid seeking help because she fears that the lymphoedema symptoms are an indicator that the cancer has recurred. Women who have lymphoedema report that the condition is debilitating.

For example, performing ordinary tasks becomes difficult and psychological distress may be experienced. The presence of other arm symptoms including weakness, limitation in range of movement, stiffness and pain also have a negative impact on quality of life for women with breast cancer. A recent study suggests that coping with lymphoedema is affected by the presence of pain and the availability of social support, as well as the severity of physical symptoms. Inquiring about the presence of arm swelling or other symptoms is important, with clinical assessment and referral, as necessary. Women may benefit from education about the early symptoms of lymphoedema and the availability of treatment.

Cognitive problems

Impaired thinking, described as poor concentration, confusion or memory problems, is a common symptom reported anecdotally by women with breast cancer, which can be especially distressing. Few detailed studies have been conducted to confirm these experiences using valid and reliable neuropsychological tests. In one such study, women with early stage breast cancer were assessed, on average, six months after adjuvant chemotherapy was completed.The study found that 75 per cent of women had moderate impairment in multiple aspects of cognitive functioning.

Difficulties observed included attention, concentration, memory and mental flexibility. Determining causality is often problematic, particularly for subtle impairment that may be a sign of treatment side effects, metastatic disease or symptomatic of an anxiety or depressive conditions or fatigue. Additional longitudinal research is needed in this area to determine prevalence, natural course and causal factors associated with cognitive impairment.

Women vary in their emotional responses to the circumstances surrounding the diagnosis and treatment of breast cancer. A woman's level of distress may also change over time. The response required by members of the treatment team to a women's emotional disturbance also varies, and is often determined by the extent to which the woman feels able to manage her emotions and how much these concerns impair her daily living. It can be part of the normal range of responses to a stressful event to experience episodically intense, unpleasant and distressing emotions such as tearfulness, being frightened and anger. These reactions are very common, are usually occasional, tend to be time-limited, rarely lasting more than a day or two, and are not inappropriate responses to significant health concerns.

The woman's existing coping strategies, as well as the provision of appropriate information, reassurance, and emotional support from the treatment team, family and support groups are useful strategies for dealing with these emotional responses. Stress and adjustment problems include stronger feelings that can last for a week or more, and these can be difficult and disruptive to a woman's life. Despite this, most women still exercise some control and can continue to function well enough. However, if such problems are left undetected and unacknowledged, some can develop into more serious emotional states.

Major psychological disturbances include a major depressive episode, anxiety disorder, or an emotional, behavioural or cognitive state that is overwhelming, lasts longer than a couple of weeks, causes significant impairment in functioning and over which the woman feels she has little or no control.

Stress and adjustment reactions

Stress and adjustment reactions describe a moderate level of emotional and psychological disturbance that includes significant symptoms of anxiety and depression. However, these are either time-limited or do not have as great an impact on functioning as disorders such as a major depressive episode. Between a quarter and a third of women will experience moderate stress and adjustment problems as a result of their diagnosis and treatment.

An Australian study demonstrated that 29 per cent of women suffered from significant adjustment problems and had depressive and/or anxiety symptoms at 3 months post-surgery. There is however, insufficient longitudinal data to describe the longterm course of significant adjustment problems in women with breast cancer. Women may be particularly vulnerable to high levels of stress at the following times:

— at diagnosis or disease recurrence;

— when facing the prospect of having surgery, be it mastectomy or breastconserving;

— during adjuvant therapy;

— around the time of medical check up; and

— living with advanced breast cancer.

Adjustment problems compromise psychological health, functioning and quality of life. Referral of women experiencing adjustment problems for appropriate intervention may prevent the development of more enduring or disabling emotional disturbances, such as depression. Appropriate interventions include cognitive behavioural, supportive or psycho-educational interventions.

Anxiety

Although some anxiety in response to a stressful life event is normal, in some cases anxiety can interfere with relationships, social or occupational functioning and health-related behaviours. Symptoms associated with anxiety include heightened physical arousal, sleep disturbance, impaired concentration and decision-making, agitation and anger. Avoidance of distressing issues and situations, and excessive reassurance-seeking, may also indicate anxiety problems. These responses can have a major impact on the woman as well as her family's functioning.

When anxiety problems become severe, specialist treatment may be required. Severe problems may include panic attacks, pervasive and generalised worry, treatment phobias (eg needle phobias), social anxiety and post-traumatic stress reactions. Estimates of the prevalence of anxiety problems among women with breast cancer range from 12 per cent to 30 per cent.

Anxiety disorders in women with breast cancer may be related to a number of different factors. These include: reaction to the stress of the diagnosis and treatment; response to cancer-related medical problems, such as uncontrolled pain; response to drug treatment, such as steroids; response to investigations, such as CT scans and MRI; and specific fears and phobias (eg needle phobias), which existed before the cancer diagnosis, but which have been exacerbated by it.

Anxiety may also be a symptom of other medical conditions, such as thyroid disease, and is commonly associated with alcohol or benzodiazepine withdrawal. When talking to women with breast cancer about their concerns and psychological well-being, it is helpful to ask specifically about anxiety. For example: 'Not surprisingly, many women with breast cancer experience some level of anxiety.

Cognitive and behavioural techniques have been demonstrated to be effective in the treatment of anxiety.

Depression

The key symptoms of depression include low or flat mood or a loss of interest in things that used to be enjoyable. The diagnosis of a major depressive episode in physically healthy patients relies heavily on symptoms such as anorexia, insomnia, anergia, fatigue, weight loss and reduced interest in sex, but in cancer patients, these symptoms may also be related to the disease process or treatment side-effects.

Thus, a diagnosis of a major depressive episode in patients is best evaluated by the severity of depressed mood, loss of interest and pleasure, the degree of feelings of hopelessness, guilt and worthlessness, and the presence of suicidal thoughts. Another symptom, recurrent tearfulness is often accompanied by social withdrawal and loss of motivation. The woman may feel she is unable to control the negative feelings and these feelings begin to dominate the day, on most days for two weeks or more.

Suicide may be a risk for the severely depressed woman. Risk factors for suicide include severely depressed mood, a family history of completed suicide, past history of self-harm and a history of alcohol or other substance abuse. Lack of any hope for the future is a risk factor for suicide. There is no evidence that asking about suicidal thoughts will prompt them in someone who had not previously considered the possibility of suicide.

Sensitive exploration of suicidal thoughts, plans and access to means is crucial. Urgent psychiatric consultation should be considered for any woman who appears at risk of suicide.

Major Psychological Disturbances

Clinicians should routinely ask about, and document, risk factors which have been found to predict adverse psychological outcomes. These include: young age at onset of disease; having children under 21 years of age; economic adversity; psychiatric history; poor social support, poor family and/or marital functioning; cumulative stressful life events; and increased treatment sideeffects.

Monitoring risk factors and anxiety and depression symptoms may assist in early identification of serious psychological disturbance. Screening for the nature and severity of psychological distress should also be done in consultations at times of diagnosis and recurrence. Based on more general research about clinical depression, early diagnosis can lead to more effective treatment outline recommended procedures for the routine screening of women for psychological problems.

Referring women for psychological treatment

There are a range of referral sources for the clinician who is concerned about the emotional well-being of the woman and/or her family members. Most oncology wards have a social worker who has expertise in counselling cancer patients, as well as practical knowledge which may be of value to women and their families. An increasing number of oncology services also have access to a clinical psychologist who is either employed directly by the oncology unit or in the hospital's Department of Psychology.

Most large metropolitan hospitals also have a psychiatric consultation-liaison service, staffed by psychiatrists, clinical psychologists, registered mental health nurses and sometimes occupational therapists who are qualified in counselling. These services exist not only to assess medically ill patients with mental illness, but also to provide assessment and advice about interventions for those coping with debilitating or life-threatening illness.

In many cases, these services can arrange appropriate longer-term follow-up, if that is indicated.

For those who work within the private health sector, the lack of ready access to an existing multi-disciplinary team may mean that provision of psychosocial support for women poses some difficulty. Given the significant contribution of psychosocial factors to overall quality of life, it is crucial that those clinicians are sensitive to the psychosocial needs of women. All clinicians need to develop their own referral network for supportive care. This would comprise individuals with expertise in the areas of breast cancer (eg psychiatrists, clinical psychologists and/or social workers) with whom they feel able to communicate about their patients.

A number of studies have evaluated the impact of providing various types of counselling or psychological interventions to women diagnosed with breast cancer. Psychosocial interventions may include, cognitive-behavioural therapy, psychotherapy, psycho-educational therapy, group therapy, and family and/or couple therapy.

In a meta-analysis of 45 randomised controlled trials with adults with cancer, those receiving psychological therapies had on average a significant improvement of 12 per cent in emotional adjustment, 10 per cent in social functioning, 14 per cent in treatment and disease-related symptoms, and 14 per cent in overall improvement in their quality of life compared to those not receiving psychological therapy.

In most trials, the therapy was provided by a specially trained counsellor, nurse, social worker or psychologist. However, greater effects have been demonstrated when psychological therapies were conducted by more highly trained therapists and continued for longer periods of time.Otherwise, trials comparing the relative effectiveness of different types of psychological interventions have indicated that most therapies have a similar effect.

All women with breast cancer should be informed that counselling is available for those who request it or who have particular needs. Choice of psychological therapy is always individually determined, dependant on the issues at hand and the skills of the therapist. Therapies may be delivered individually, or via a group or family model. While some women will be more comfortable with the privacy of individual counselling, other women will benefit from group counselling where they can gain from sharing the commonality of their experience.

The use of medication for psychological disturbance in women with breast cancer. In many instances a psychiatrist will initiate treatment with these medications. It is important for all members of the treatment team to recognise the potential role of medication as part of the comprehensive treatment of psychological disturbance in women with breast cancer.

In many cases in oncology, the management of acute anxiety states and anxiety disorders requires pharmacotherapy in addition to relaxation or other psychological interventions. The drugs used for treatment of anxiety include benzodiazepines, antipsychotics, antihistamines and antidepressants. Choice of a particular agent depends on the acuteness or chronicity of the anxiety state, the drug's absorption rate, the available route for administration, concurrent medical problems and drug side-effects.

— *Benzodiazepines*: These are the mainstay of pharmacological treatment of acute anxiety. Shorter-acting benzodiazepines, such as alprazolam, are safest but there may be breakthrough anxiety, necessitating substitution with a longer-acting benzodiazepine, such as diazepam. For those with hepatic disease, drugs such as oxazepam are safest. Long term use of benzodiazepines has been associated with dependence. Benzodiazepines should never be ceased abruptly because of the risk of withdrawal symptoms, which may include seizures.

— *Neuroleptics*: In cases of extreme agitation, low doses of antipsychotics, such as thioridazine or haloperidol may be used, bearing in mind the risk of extrapyramidal side-effects. Depression The optimal management of a major depressive episode in women with breast cancer should incorporate a combination of supportive psychotherapy, cognitive and behavioural techniques, and pharmacotherapy. The concern that antidepressant therapy poses an unacceptable side-effect burden, is not supported by research.

— *Tricyclic antidepressants*: The tricyclic antidepressants have been used for many years for the treatment of depression. Their sedating properties are particularly useful for management of the agitated, depressed person with insomnia.Their potentiation and enhancement of opioid analgesia is also useful for those with pain. Anticholinergic side-effects may aggravate stomatitis secondary to chemotherapy and may exacerbate constipation. These drugs also have the potential to affect cardiac rhythm. Cancer patients may respond to tricyclic antidepressants at a lower dose than physically healthy people.

— *Selective serotonin reuptake inhibitors (SSRIs)*: Unlike the tricyclic antidepressants, the SSRIs are a newer class of drugs, and there have been fewer studies of their effectiveness in cancer patients. The SSRIs have fewer anticholinergic or cardiovascular side-effects and are less sedating than the tricyclic antidepressants, but may be associated with some exacerbation of anxiety or insomnia. Nausea may be a limiting sideeffect in cancer patients. The potential for drug interactions, such as with warfarin, may limit the use of SSRIs.

— *Selective noradrenergic reuptake inhibitors (SNRIs):* New agents, like venlafaxine, provide both selective noradrenergic and serotonergic reuptake inhibition, with fewer anticholinergic, histaminic, adrenergic effects, and no monoamine oxidase inhibition. They are likely to have a helpful role in cancer care.

— *Psychostimulants:* Limited research suggests that patients with advanced cancer may experience some improvement in depressed mood, appetite and well-being when treated with low-dose psychostimulants. Sideeffects include nervousness, over-stimulation, mild increases in blood pressure and pulse rate, and tremor. Long-term use of these drugs is associated with tolerance and dependence.

5

Ethics in Psychotherapy and Counselling

In recent years there has been a growth in interest and concern about the field of ethics and values for many reasons. In the second half of the twentieth century, after the Second World War, there was a consensus in which the common good was seen to be service to all citizens. In the UK this was expressed, for example, in the terms of the National Health Service and the Education Act 1944.

In the 1980s, attitudes were changed and the emphasis moved from the practitioner who was offering the service to the rights of citizens receiving it. The language changed to stress the rights of consumers, thus patients became customers. Words like accountability acquired much greater importance in political and social life. Professionals who had assumed that they knew what was best for the patient began to have to explain what they were doing and why, both to their colleagues and to the public.

Richard Rowson, has pointed out that there is no clear distinction to be made between ethics and morals.

However, the main difference in common usage would be perhaps that morals are usually seen as the system adopted by an individual whereas ethics is the science of morality or of duty. Values are the expression of the esteem with which a person or society regards an object and it is with this esteem or valuing that we are mainly concerned.

The editors have both served on various professional ethics committees and are well aware of the complexity of the questions that may arise in the professional setting leading to a request for help or advice. The work that a psychotherapist does is of great significance. Though we have the power to do good, we also have the power to do ill. Most of the models in use today would place a high value on such concepts as awareness and choice, and perhaps increasingly also on responsibility and an attitude of concern for others.

Psychoanalytic theory and the forms of therapy that have grown from it, or in reaction to it, have not had a great deal to say explicitly about ethics and values. Nevertheless, every aspect of developmental theory or psychopathology implies a view of human nature and of the way in which we value some behaviours, character structures and states of mind as being better or worse than others.

Therapists span a wide range in their views of the purpose of their work, all the way from the therapeutic zealot who sets out to heal and cure humanity to the freelance philosopher who has no intention beyond seeking to encourage learning and thinking. In the middle of this range would be those who take a developmental view and consider that they are facilitating forward movement that had become blocked in some way. Even the most minimalist of these views would require valuing one thing more than another.

Most therapists, if pressed, could come up with some aphorisms to convey the goals of their work: to make the unconscious conscious, to replace id with ego, to develop the capacity to reflect, to reach the 'depressive position' at least some of the time, to have better relationships with oneself or others. This is just a sample but it already introduces words like 'better', which raise the question: who decides what is better? If we pay some sort of homage to the overarching value of autonomy, then we would hope that the client or patient would be developing a personal view of what is good or better.

Each individual therapist must face his or her own values in the process of theory making and technique building. Values are formed and hardened by the culture and groups surrounding us and the outcomes of certain behaviour in contrast with other sorts. In recent years therapists have been made aware of the judgements that have been made by individuals and groups about the worth of what we do. The United Kingdom Council for Psychotherapy (UKCP) has issued a resource document for practitioners, that emphasizes the importance of agnosticism in dealing with questions of the accuracy of memories and the problems that arise from lending particular weight to an account that is given, at one particular moment in a therapy, about what happened in the past. Therapists will of course take seriously the emotional needs of the patient who is recounting any history and particularly one that involves abuse or violence.

A major area of value formation and influence is in the field of difference and equal opportunities. Both outside and inside the profession, there is great concern about ethics and standards. This ranges from an interest in moral philosophy to a deep concern about the pressures that colleagues in the statutory and voluntary sectors can find themselves facing in relation to ethics and values. Similarly the commercial world, police, press and the churches have found themselves the subject of scrutiny in these areas.

As religious affiliation and practice decline there is a countervailing growth in public interest in ethical questions coming from every facet of society. These concerns reflect and are reflected in a profound interest in the inner and outer work of psychotherapists. There are, however, few books that deal with this subject. Tim Bond has written on the practical aspect of ethics in Standards and Ethics for Counsellors in Action and Jeremy Holmes and Richard Lindley (1989) on The Values of Psychotherapy. The popularity of both of these books indicates the need for a basis for discussion and thought about some of the more contentious and subtle aspects of values in the work of psychotherapy. Alan Tjeltveit (1999) in Ethics and Values in Psychotherapy considers the philosophical basis for establishing values.

Richard Rowson gives the philosopher's view of academic ethics as a study of morality and establishes some definitions. Del Loewenthal, Robert Snell and Petruska Clarkson consider the therapist's responsibility to the other and the morality of intervening or not intervening, taking up or repudiating the bystander's position. The next four chapters recognize that any attempt to consider the value system of the therapist must pay attention to the way that the therapist's values are expressed in the process and technique that is actually used in the consulting room. Josephine Klein discusses the process of assessment where subjective and value judgements are inevitably a part. She suggests ways in which the values of the assessor may be recognized more openly and may be more helpful to the patient. Once the process has begun other areas of tension arise.

David Mann writes about the values that are involved in dealing with erotic transference and countertransference. Fiona Palmer Barnes considers the impasses that arise when the ordinary processes of therapy are not enough to enable movement. Psychotherapists recognize that the work affects those in the immediate and wider environment of the client.

Psychotherapy does not take place in a closed container. The social context will inevitably affect the way in which we work in the sessions and also the kinds of constraints and demands that we have to face both inside and outside the consulting room. Thus community and culture affect the patient, the therapist and the work that we do. Mark Aveline considers the dilemmas raised by such issues as confidentiality and the risk of harm and self-harm.

The ethical principles to which we subscribe personally may or may not be compatible with our legal system, or the codes of our profession, since they are independent of them. They may, however, be dependent on any religious beliefs we hold.

For over 2500 years people have debated whether what is right and wrong is a matter of objective moral truth, or a matter of opinion - that is whether, when we judge someone's behaviour as right or wrong, we are describing factual aspects of their behaviour or expressing our feelings about the person's behaviour or reporting conventional social opinions about it.

If you are the person who makes a moral judgement, you may see it as pointing out a moral fact or stating a truth. So Jane may see herself as saying that John's behaviour actually is wrong, not merely expressing her disapproval or claiming that his behaviour flouts convention. She may support her conviction by identifying aspects of his behaviour which make it wrong: he had deliberately encouraged the patient's dependency, knowingly allowed their mutual attraction to develop, not terminated the professional relationship once the attraction became evident, and so on.

People who, by contrast, regard ethical judgements as expressing either the speaker's opinions, or the conventional attitudes of the culture to which the speaker belongs, will think that to attempt to prove moral facts shows a misunderstanding of the nature of morality. They consider that morality is not about facts or truths at all, but about values and principles which people happen to hold at a particular time in a particular culture.

Those who see judgements as expressing the speaker's opinions will regard Jane's conviction that she is stating facts about John's behaviour as simply indicating the strength of her attitude towards it: so strongly does she disapprove of what he did that its wrongness seems to be a matter of fact to her.

Those who consider that judgements express conventional attitudes will regard her conviction that she is stating a fact as evidence of how completely she has 'internalized' the attitudes of her culture. Is ethics concerned with aiming for the best consequences or with carrying out specific duties?

There are two other fundamentally different views about the nature of ethics. One - the consequentialist view

- is that ethics is concerned with bringing about the best consequences. In its simplest form, this view is that our ethical obligation is to do whatever will bring the greatest benefits to everyone. So if everyone is likely to be happier if we tell a lie rather than tell the truth, we should tell the lie.

According to this view, actions such as telling a lie or breaking promises are not intrinsically bad, nor are actions such as telling the truth and keeping promises intrinsically good. All actions are ethically neutral, and whether they are right or wrong in particular circumstances depends on whether they lead to the best consequences. The end justifies the means, and since lying is not intrinsically bad, we have no obligation to avoid doing it. Because the consequentialist perspective sees value in ends and not actions, it is often referred to as the teleological view of ethics, telos being the Greek for 'end' or 'objective'.

The other view of ethics is the dutiful or deontological view - deon being Greek for 'duty'. According to this, certain types of actions are intrinsically good, and others intrinsically bad. Our ethical duties consist in carrying out the first and avoiding the second. The actions regarded as intrinsically good vary, but generally include respecting autonomy, telling the truth, keeping promises and being just. Those regarded as intrinsically bad usually include taking life and inflicting harm.

Not everyone holds either a teleological or deontological view. Some people - referred to as ethical pluralists - hold both, considering that ethical decision making requires us to bear in mind the demands of each perspective. So if keeping a promise would harm others, when deciding what to do they would weigh the ethical importance of keeping it against the importance of not harming others.

Teleological, deontological and ethical pluralist views are all compatible with both the 'fact/truth' and 'opinion' views of morality. Someone could regard it as a fact that ethics is concerned with seeking consequences or that it is concerned with being dutiful or that it is concerned with both. Others could regard it as a matter of opinion that it is concerned with one or the other or both.

Ethical Principles

Ethical principles means the rules which people are committed to because they see them as embodying their values and justifying their moral judgements. When people make moral judgements we normally expect them to be able to justify them. Some people are committed to only one fundamental principle: utilitarians, for example, think that the principle of utility should be the sole basis for our judgements.

Deontologists, on the other hand, subscribe to more than one principle - such as tell the truth, respect autonomy and keep promises -but they reject the principle of utility, while ethical pluralists accept several principles, including the principle of utility. Whatever principles people hold, they may see them as part of a 'fact' or 'opinion' view of morality. So someone may regard it as a fact that morality is based solely on the principle of utility, or may consider that it is so in their opinion, or in the conventional opinion of their culture. Similarly an ethical pluralist or deontologist may regard it as a matter of fact or opinion that morality is based on several ethical principles.

The principle of utility

The principle of utility underlies Sally's view. She judges the value of actions by their utility in bringing about valuable consequences. For her it is the consequences of John's behaviour that make it right, irrespective of its nature. Within professional contexts this principle is frequently interpreted as the requirement to seek the best interests of our clients. However, its demands are wider than this, and require us to bear in mind the interests of everyone - including ourselves - who might be affected by our actions. The principle of utility is applied in two basic forms.

One, act utilitarianism, considers that before we act we should assess the likely outcomes of all options and choose whichever act we think will be the most beneficial in the particular circumstances. The other, rule utilitarianism, considers that we should formulate rules we think would lead to the most beneficial consequences if everyone were to follow them in all relevantly similar circumstances. According to utilitarians, when calculating which actions or rules would be most beneficial, we should consider the likely long-term effects. Many think we should not consider the effects just on humans, born and unborn, but on all sentient life - animals, birds, insects, fish and even plants.

Moreover, since most actions and rules are likely to cause some harm as well as benefits, we should choose whichever we think will result in the greatest net benefit over harm. By accepting the principle of utility as the basis for our ethical decisions we take on tremendous responsibilities. For, in order to calculate benefits and harms as thoroughly as we can, we must be as well informed as possible, not only about how our decisions might affect others, but also how they might feel about these effects. In so far as our actions can affect clients and colleagues, we must therefore understand as well as we can their preferences, priorities and perspectives.

We must also be as impartial as possible. We must, for example, allocate resources - our time, professional expertise and money - solely on the criterion of what will produce the greatest net benefit, and not give priority to some people over others just because we have greater affinity to them. As utilitarians we must regard the well-being of people we do not know as just as important ethically as the well-being of those we do, even though they are less important to us emotionally.

Many people applaud this stance of impartiality. Because it regards the suffering and well-being of people and creatures who are not members of particular group - our family, gender, age group, nationality, race, creed or species - as important as similar levels of suffering and well-being of those who are, it is anti-sexist, anti-ageist, anti-racist and anti-speciesist.

Some people also find another aspect of this principle unacceptable. Since maximization of benefit is its only aim, we are obliged by it to ignore any wishes and interests of individuals which are likely to prevent us achieving the greatest net benefit over harm. We should therefore ignore clients' wishes and not seek their welfare if we are certain we can bring about better consequences by doing something else. We might, for instance, decide to provide no therapy for people over the age of 70, if research indicates that greater benefit for the whole population can be achieved by allocating all our resources to younger people.

Moreover, as utilitarians we should have no moral scruples in doing this, since we consider that fair allocation of resources has no intrinsic value. It has value only if it happens to lead to greater net benefit. Considerations such as these lead deontologists to reject completely the principle of utility as a basis for moral judgements. Ethical pluralists accept that its demands have some ethical legitimacy, so include it as one of the principles on which they base their judgements, but they restrain its teleological demands by one or more of the deontological principles.

So they may consider that although we have a prima facie obligation to seek the greatest net benefit overall, we should weigh the importance of this against the importance of carrying out such deontological principles as respecting autonomy, telling the truth, keeping promises, respecting confidentiality, treating people fairly and justly, and not causing harm. A prima facie obligation is one we should fulfil unless the ethical value of doing so is outweighed by the ethical value of meeting some other obligation. In contrast, an absolute obligation is one we should always fulfil, come what may.

Autonomy

Autonomy' means being self-determining, that is making one's own decisions about which ethical views and beliefs one will hold and about how one will live - for example, a patient deciding which therapies to pursue. We respect the autonomy of others, first, by enabling them to make such decisions, and second, by not overriding their decisions once made. The principle of respecting autonomy underpins widely accepted views on human rights, which are primarily concerned to promote and protect the self-determination of individuals.

A powerful strand in western culture is the view that a supremely valuable attribute of humans is their capacity to make moral choices and take moral responsibility for their actions. We achieve our full dignity and worth as human beings only when we exercise this capacity. Our ethical concern should therefore be to promote and protect this capacity in ourselves and others. The principle of respecting autonomy forbids using people for our own ends. If we do this we treat 'persons', who are supremely valuable, as 'things', that is, as objects which are valuable to us only as tools to enable us achieve what we want.

Even if what we want is admirable - such as to benefit others as much as we can - we should not manipulate other people to achieve it. In this way the demand that we respect autonomy is a bulwark against the paternalism of utilitarianism. Consequently, many people regard respect for patients' autonomy as vital in professional relationships. To enable clients to be autonomous we should be truthful with them about their situation. If we have information relevant to a decision they have to make, we should give it to them as fully and impartially as we can. We should try to make their decision well informed and as uninfluenced by our values as possible and, when they have made their decision, we should not interfere with it.

Some people conclude that we are not entitled to override autonomous decisions which affect only the person who makes them, although we may override other people's autonomous decisions if they would harm others against their will. Such interference is seen as justified because it protects the autonomy of those who would otherwise be harmed.

However others challenge this, claiming that we have no moral obligation to ensure that other people respect the autonomy of third parties, only to ensure we respect it ourselves - even if this results in us not interfering with decisions which are likely to harm others. So if another psychotherapist does not respect her patient's autonomy, that is her moral failure, not mine. It would be my failure if I did not respect her decision about how to treat her patient.

Like respect for autonomy, these principles intimately affect the way we conduct professional relationships. Some people see them as deontological principles - that is, as prescribing actions which are intrinsically valuable -hence our duty to perform them. Some see them as utilitarian rules - that is, as rules we should generally follow because, on the whole, abiding by them brings greater benefit than not doing so. On this view communities, human relationships and professional activities are more successful if participants can rely on each other telling the truth and doing what they say they will do.

Equally, professional objectives are more likely to be achieved if clients communicate openly with psychotherapists and counsellors, and they will do so if they can trust that confidentiality will be kept. People have different views on the relative importance of these three principles. Some, for example, consider we should keep information confidential whatever the circumstances, while others think that although confidentiality is valuable in itself, its value can be outweighed by other duties. So in certain circumstances - say an inquiry into professional misconduct - the duty of confidentiality may be less important than the duty to tell the truth. Just as there are different views as to what is necessary to respect autonomy, so there are in relation to telling the truth, keeping promises and respecting confidentiality.

Some people think that to tell the truth we must give information about everything we know which may be relevant. Others think that we may choose what to tell and what not to tell and that, provided we have not uttered a lie, we have not flouted the principle to tell the truth. A practitioner is aware that her patient is adopted. There are similar variations as to what is thought necessary to keep a promise.

Although for many people this is the most important of ethical principles, it is dealt with only briefly here as it is unlikely to be a major consideration in psychotherapy and counselling. Some people consider that we have an absolute obligation not to take human life - whatever the circumstances we are never justified in deliberately destroying it. Others see it as a prima facie obligation: it is wrong to take life but we may sometimes be justified in doing so, the onus being on anyone who takes life to justify it by citing exceptional circumstances. These may, for instance, be that the taking of life was the unintended but unavoidable result of acting in self-defence, or that it was the just punishment of a convicted murderer.

There is a spectrum of views as to what type of 'human life' is so supremely valuable that it should not be taken. At one end is the conviction that every form of life - from the fertilized ovum to the brain-dead body kept alive by artificial means - has the same supreme worth.

At the other end is the view that the only humans who have this value are those who are self-aware, have expectation for their future and can relate to others. There are also different perceptions as to what constitutes 'taking' life. For some we take life only if we deliberately do something positive to terminate it: say, administer a lethal injection. For others we take life if we merely withdraw life-prolonging treatment or if we fail to intervene when a life is under threat: if we do not, for example, give warmth and sustenance to a newborn baby.

The principle not to cause harm - known as the principle of non-maleficence - is seen by many as vital to professional care: before all else, we have a duty to ensure we do not harm our clients. Some who think in terms of a hierarchy of duties see the duty not to cause harm as one of - if not the - most important of all. Next in importance is the duty to prevent or remove harm, followed by the positive duty to create beneficial results. So we should not attempt to benefit anyone until we are certain we shall not cause them any harm.

According to this view the duty not to cause harm is absolute and the principle of non-maleficence must overrule the utilitarian view that it is acceptable to cause harm if doing so will achieve the greatest net benefit over harm. Of course what is meant by 'harm' varies enormously. It can be destruction of life, physical and psychological suffering, unjust treatment and failure to respect autonomy. The wider one's interpretation of 'harm', the fewer courses of action will be seen to cause no harm whatsoever.

Consequently in professional situations many people find it difficult to accept the principle of non-maleficence as giving an absolute duty, and regard it as permissible to balance benefits against harm. However, if a patient is not able to make an autonomous decision, we may be faced with a dilemma arising from the clashing principles of non-maleficence and utility.

Treat people fairly and justly

Fairness and justice have many meanings, but in relation to psychotherapy and counselling we can interpret what is meant by treating people fairly and justly as:

— we treat people fairly when we treat them alike unless some relevant difference between them requires us to treat them differently and

— we treat people justly when we treat each individual 'according to his/her due'.

Since to be fair we should treat people alike unless there is a relevant difference between them, we should not treat differently clients who have the same problem but who differ in gender, race, sexual orientation, age, religion or nationality unless these differences actually affect what treatment is appropriate for them as individuals. The problem, of course, lies in identifying which attributes of individuals we should take into account when deciding whether it is fair treat them differently and what is justly due to each person.

Those aspects most frequently identified in relation to the provision of psychotherapy and counselling are needs and deserts: individuals who have greater needs, or are more deserving, should be given greater resources or greater priority. But to make just decisions on this basis we need impartial and agreed criteria by which to compare needs and deserts, and these are hard to establish. One suggestion is that certain things are fundamental to the well-being of us all.

These things - such as a sufficient amount of food and warmth - are our basic needs, and those who do not have them are in greater need than those who do. The difficulty with this approach, however, is that it provides us with a basis for decision making only in the most extreme circumstances. For, beyond having common needs for enough food, clothing and warmth to keep us alive, we vary enormously as to what else is essential for our individual well-being.

Some intellectuals do not seem to need such relationships, but they do need calm states of mind to pursue their interests. So the self-sufficient intellectual seeking help to overcome panic attacks may be in just as great a need for therapy as someone who cannot form good relationships. In view of such considerations some people do not see basic needs as specific things we all require, but as whatever is essential to the well-being of particular individuals.

However, since what is necessary for the well-being of each of us can vary enormously, this can result in some people being entitled to disproportionate amounts of resources. Moreover, this approach also makes it difficult to distinguish 'needs' from 'wants', yet many people see this distinction as a useful way of separating more important desires from less important ones. Without such a distinction, we may feel obliged to meet those requirements of an individual which seem trivial or, again, disproportionately demanding. We are then faced with whether it is fair to give much more to some than to others.

On the other hand, if we do make the distinction between needs and wants we can be accused of unjustly imposing our values on others by regarding some of their desires as 'mere wants'. In the following cases individuals suffer similar levels of unhappiness and poor self-esteem because of disappointed expectations. They each ask for help in overcoming their difficulties.

The idea that we should live in accord with nature is similarly powerful: so much so that for some people merely to refer to something as 'unnatural' is enough to imply that it is wrong. But though powerful and pervasive, the appeal to nature is notoriously vague and so open to a variety of interpretations and questionable claims. One appeal to 'nature as a whole' as the arbiter of what is right and wrong is based on the idea that nature is a system in which the various components have specific functions to perform. By carrying out their specific functions the components enable the objectives of the whole system to be achieved.

From an impartial observation of the facts of nature alone, we cannot claim that sexual activities have only one specific function since we see them used for a variety of functions: expressions of affection, as re-enforcements of relationships and as recreation. To justify the claim that sexual activity should be used for only one purpose we must, then, appeal to some other values or beliefs we hold. One such belief may be that nature is created by a mind-or God-who intends sexuality to be used in only one way. However, if this is the ground for our view we cannot claim it is founded on an objective observation of the 'facts' of nature alone.

Similar problems arise if by 'nature' people mean 'human nature', since how we see human nature and what we regard as the function of human beings are also influenced by the cultural values and religious beliefs we hold. Furthermore, whatever our conception of human nature, we are likely to see it as complex, and this obscures any clear guidance we might seek by appealing to 'human nature'. For most people think humans normally have both emotions and the ability to reason and we act in accord with the former if we react emotionally and spontaneously, and in accord with the latter if we calculate what it is best to do before we act.

But when emotions and reasons clash, which should we follow? The claim that either is the more fundamental part of our nature, and so the one we should always follow, is difficult to maintain. And if it is claimed we should follow whichever we think appropriate in the circumstances, we need values other than simply the principle 'live in accord with human nature' by which to decide which is appropriate.

Another interpretation of 'acting in accord with human nature' is 'doing what the majority does'. A difficulty with this is that 'what the majority does' varies from culture to culture and decade to decade. Moreover the claim that an activity is unnatural and wrong because only a minority do it is indefensible unless it is applied consistently to all minority activities. For anyone who regards only some minority activities as wrong must have other values or principles by which to judge some activities and not others as unacceptable. But, in fact, no one does apply the principle consistently, since no one regards all minority activities - collecting train numbers, being a concert pianist or psychotherapist, for example - as unnatural and wrong.

People who, for instance, claim that homosexuality or interracial marriages are unnatural and wrong because only a minority engage in them, do not condemn all other minority activities. They must therefore have some other values or beliefs they hold to give plausibility to their condemnation of these particular activities.

In the nineteenth and twentieth centuries, and especially since the United Nations Declaration of Human

Rights of 1948, the concept of 'rights' has become increasingly important in ethical thinking.

There are different types of rights - legal, institutional and moral. How do they differ? Legal and institutional rights are entitlements that people possess by virtue of living under, or belonging to, a particular legal system or institution. For example, legal systems may give people the legal right to travel on the public highway, and universities give fee-paying students the institutional right to use the library. Whether or not someone has such rights is a matter of fact which can be ascertained by checking the relevant laws and rules.

In contrast, claims about moral rights, including human and natural rights, are based on moral viewpoints which cannot be checked to be true or false like statements of fact. For instance, if people assert that women have a moral right to abortion on demand, their claim is based on their particular ethical principles and the way that they prioritize them. They may in this case consider that respect for autonomy is more important than respect for life in the form of the human foetus.

'Natural' and 'human' rights are moral rights based on what people see human nature as being. John Locke, for instance, in his Two Treatises of Government (1690), claimed that the enjoyment of one's property is a natural right, because he thought it part of human nature to live in societies in which individuals own personal property. Others, however, have pointed out that there is no idea of personal property in some societies, and so the right to enjoy one's personal property can, at most, be claimed to be a right in certain cultures, not a universal natural right. Similar challenges are made to the claim that the United Nations Declaration of 1948 is a statement of universal rights.

Although claims about moral, human and natural rights express moral viewpoints, they are often assumed to be stating objective and unquestionable facts for two reasons. First, because statements about legal and institutional rights are about facts, many people who do not distinguish between different types of rights assume moral rights are also about facts. Second, because claims about all types of rights have the linguistic form of statements, they are often understood as stating facts.

In some countries, however, statements of human rights have become embodied into legislation. In the UK, for example, the Human Rights Act now embodies the European Convention on Human Rights into law. Where this has happened statements of human rights reflect legal facts.

As Tjeltveit notes: 'When psychotherapists assert that they are professionals, they announce, they profess, they make public testimony that they possess specialized knowledge and technical skills that help people with psychological problems.' A promise is made that the profession can be trusted to act in other than.its own interests, so an ideology of public service and altruism is espoused. Hence the assertion of professional status implies both competence, in specialized knowledge and skills, and ethical commitment.

Of course, these claims are made by the emerging profession on its own behalf and in conjunction with the formation of a professional body representing its interests. So, against the ideal of altruism we must set the recognition that, since their origins, initially as law, medicine and the clergy, in the medieval universities, professions have been characterized by the monopolization of particular forms of expertise and the erection of social boundaries around themselves. They control entry through lengthy training and qualifications and are thus as much about exclusion and power as about service.

Professional power has long been the subject of critiques from both left and right political perspectives and the demand for regulation can be seen both as a negative manifestation of power and as a genuine acknowledgement of, and desire to redress, abuses of power. Ethical frameworks, codes of practice and disciplinary procedures are, in part, aspects of selfregulation that serve to establish trust, by ensuring some protection for clients. They can thus be situated alongside legal and political frameworks, and ethical, legal and political issues inevitably interrelate.

Professionalization in the UK, as elsewhere, has had a complex history, marked by dissent, and resulting here in the formation of not one but four main professional bodies. Although evolving from earlier organizations, three have been established within the past 30 years: the British Association for Counselling and Psychotherapy; the United Kingdom Standing Conference (1989)/ Council (1992) for Psychotherapy; and, the British Confederation of Psychotherapists (1992).

The British Psychological Society has a longer history, being established in 1901 and incorporated by Royal Charter in 1965. However, it did not register chartered psychologists until 1987 and counselling psychologists were not chartered until 1992. It is now beginning to register chartered psychologists specializing in psychotherapy. The BACP and the BPS are membership organizations, whereas the UKCP and the BCP are umbrella organizations. Practitioners of therapy may be called counsellors, psychotherapists, counselling or clinical psychologists.

So, particularly in moving towards regulation, the question has arisen as to whether we are talking about one or a number of different professions or perhaps one or two different kinds of activity (counselling and psychotherapy) that differing professions (including psychology and psychiatry) all practise. Each professional body commits practitioners to ethical standards and codes of practice. The main concerns, in the context of selfregulation, are to protect clients/patients from bad practice, and with the ethos and conditions within which therapy takes place. To this end there is significant agreement across the codes about basic principles and standards of conduct.

Ethical issues are seen largely as relating to aspects of conduct, such as the management of boundaries and the non-exploitation of clients, and to dilemmas arising in situations where values conflict, for example those of client autonomy and client safety. However, such issues, relating to the standards and conditions of practice, may be seen as external to the actual process of therapy, which is often, though not always, conceived in psychological rather than ethical terms. This is reflected in the way that ethics is often approached on training courses, with codes of ethics and practice being introduced but not discussed in depth.

Training focuses on what is seen as the theory and practice of the approach or approaches to therapy itself. The way that the codes have been written, as rules, has no doubt contributed to this marginalization of ethical thinking. Nevertheless, in the context of professionalization, ethics has begun to feature more significantly in the curriculum, usually as the kinds of issue and dilemma noted above. Moreover, the BACP has recently developed a fundamentally changed ethical framework and the BPS is engaged in a similar task.

These two major professional bodies are moving away from an approach to professional conduct based on sets of rules, towards one based on values and principles. This will require those of us whose practice they govern to think differently about ethics. It will take time to establish, but the change is quite profound. Ethical thinking and reasoned judgements based on values and principles will be expected and there will be less specific guidance in the form of rules.

Moreover, at least within the BACP framework, which draws as much on virtue ethics as on duty ethics, practitioners will be expected to cultivate personal qualities, such as empathy, sincerity and respect, considered to be characteristic of good therapists, as a matter of ethical responsibility as well as in the context of technical competence. This emphasis on personal qualities and values reorients the approach to professional ethics in a way that makes ethical thinking central to the process of therapy.

Ashcroft notes, in an article introducing the new framework, that it does so precisely by drawing attention to the personal and moral qualities of the practitioner and stressing the personal dimension and the quality of the relationship in therapy. He states unequivocally that, 'Counselling and psychotherapy are thoroughly ethical activities, in the deepest sense of the term "ethical". They are concerned with the process of discovering the good life'. Thus, in his view, the new framework defines therapy as a fundamentally ethical activity.

Of course, there are differing aspects of, and ways of characterizing, ethics. Bohme distinguishes three:

— A branch of academic philosophy, an area of knowledge of a specific kind with its own methods and schools.

— Connected with the idea of philosophy as a mode of living or a way of life.

— Practical wisdom.

Ashcroft is clearly linking therapy with the second, where ethical or moral questions are seen as arising when matters become serious for each of us individually. Bohme argues that how we decide those questions determines who we are and how we regard ourselves. They are questions that have to do with 'being-human-well' or virtue ethics. The third characterization of ethics, as practical wisdom, centres on public as distinct from personal concerns. Here the basic values of communal life are at issue and arguments involve the formation of public opinion as a background for social regulation. So ethical or moral questions arise when matters become serious for a community and affect how it regards itself and what it becomes. In this aspect it is easy to see the interrelationship of ethics and politics.

All this points to areas of contested, or at least shared, ground between ethics and psychology, of central relevance to therapy. Engaging with clients about issues relating to who they are and how they regard themselves is clearly an ethical activity as defined above. Moreover, ethics as practical wisdom seems to be what we engage in when we publicly debate the nature of therapy, how we regard it and what it should become, particularly in relation to regulation. On the other hand, psychological theories, explicitly or implicitly, contain normative notions about the nature of persons, their well-being and potential, and debates between theoretical approaches and models of therapy can be seen as debates within psychology.

The relationship between ethics and psychology are fundamental in defining the profession. Whereas the new BACP framework stresses the ethical character of therapy and the centrality of personal qualities and relationship, the claim to expertise and the possession of specialized knowledge and technical skills is frequently made on the basis of psychology. So the relation between ethics and psychology involves a tension which can be usefully expressed in terms of Buber's distinction between two modes of being-in-relation, 'I-It' and 'I-Thou'. This can translate into seeing ourselves, as practitioners, as either technical experts or as persons in relation.

Interestingly, there is a wealth of psychological research evidence demonstrating the therapeutic significance of the practitioner-client relationship. Roth and Fonagy clearly confirm this, and Hubble et al., in their analysis of outcome research, identify client variables and extra-therapeutic factors as accounting for as much as 40 per cent of improvement in therapy and the therapeutic relationship as accounting for 30 per cent. Placebo/ expectancy effects and specific techniques each account for 15 per cent. Moreover, the evidence that, in terms of overall effectiveness, no one therapeutic approach is better than any other is persuasive. This seems to underscore the emphasis of the BACP framework.

Nonetheless, despite the evidence, professionalization favours a stress on technical competence and an increasing reliance on therapeutic techniques. 'Doing to' is emphasized over a relationship in which 'being-with' a person is paramount; 'I-It' takes precedence over 'I-Thou' irrespective of the therapeutic approach. Lomas has, for instance, drawn attention to the increasing emphasis on technique over relationship within the psychoanalytic tradition. He explores some of the ways in which what he terms 'the retreat from the ordinary' damages the therapeutic process and diverts attention from its personal and ethical dimensions.

Of course, this seeming 'ordinariness' of 'being-in-relation' is part of the problem. It can appear to undermine the claim to professional expertise. Nevertheless, Carl Rogers, who did much to establish the significance of relationship in therapeutic processes, stressed that therapeutic relationships are not different in kind from relationships in everyday life. What can be overlooked is the intrinsic value of meeting when depth of contact can be established in the relationship. Rogers emphasized the extraordinary therapeutic potential of this ordinary human capacity and we owe much to his careful work in researching its nature and potential and for identifying such key therapeutic factors as acceptance, empathy and congruence.

Differing therapeutic approaches now draw upon this under-standing and one might expect it to lead to a more significant focus on research into the relationship and an exploration of issues that arise when this is considered in some depth. For example, while there are strong affinities between the approaches of Rogers and Buber, there are significant differences with implications for practice. It is possible, in the area of relationship, to imagine ethical and psychological inquiry as complementary. Indeed, deepening our understanding of acceptance, empathy and congruence requires this as they relate to psychological attributes and skills of the therapist, to her or his ethical virtues and to the declared values of therapeutic practice.

More commonly, the relationship is considered superficially and reduced to a precondition for the application of techniques, the 'technical expert' overshadows the 'person-in-relation'. This stress on technical expertise can be linked both to the employment context and to the way psychology has developed as a discipline, traditionally adopting a 'natural science' model.

It is favoured by professional recognition and the increasing employment of therapists in organizations where a heavy demand on resources is coupled with a justifiable expectation of accountability.

Such settings tend to promote short-term problem- or solution-focused work and standardized, manualized and even computerized treatments to the exclusion of more flexible, creative approaches and longer-term, in-depth work. There is a strong demand for evidence-based practice which encourages research conforming to the dominant 'natural science' model and a bias towards cognitive-behavioural therapy.

This best fits the model and, importantly for a profession working increasingly in medically dominated contexts, can strengthen claims to a distinctive field of psychologically defined expertise validated by research. However, much research can be criticized for being constrained by notions of good design inappropriate to complex life situations. Despite the weight of theory and research that challenges it, the 'natural science' view of modern psychology, although modified, is still mainstream and supported by a long history. Its development, in the second half of the nineteenth century, as psychology emerged as one of the disciplines aiming to study human beings scientifically, can be understood as part of a wider social and historical process, conceptualized as 'rationalization' by Weber.

Rationalization involves the application of rational decision-making criteria to increasing areas of social life and is linked with the rise of industrial capitalism in the West. Progressively freed from the external constraint of values (historically the 'Protestant ethic'), productivity becomes an end in itself as opposed to a means whereby independently identified human needs can be satisfied. The effect is to construct a complex 'iron cage' of bureaucratic rules and regulations geared to calculable economic efficiency.

Different spheres of life are increasingly separated and subject to specialization and the creation of technical experts, forming what Habermas terms 'subsystems of instrumental action'. Rationality is reduced to a single form, 'instrumental rationality', and defined entirely in terms of the most efficient means to achieve subsystem-specific goals, such as 'productivity', 'scientific truth' and 'technological progress'. Imagination, emotional experience, the arts and moral values are all effectively excluded from the sphere of reason and truth.

The model of professional practice that arises casts practitioners in the role of instrumental problem-solvers applying technical expertise to well-formed problems. Schön, in offering an alternative 'reflective practitioner' model, argues that it falsely suggests a high, hard ground overlooking a swamp. On the high ground, manageable problems lend themselves to solution through the application of research based theory and technique. In tune with the process of rationalization, in which technological and social progress are linked, traditional 'scientific' psychology is rooted in the Enlightenment philosophies of empiricism and positivism.

It stresses knowledge claims based on 'objectively observable facts' verifiable against 'sense-experience'. This emphasis on objectivity and observability favours the study of behaviour rather than subjective experience. Laws allowing the prediction and control of behaviour are sought which, once discovered, can be applied to the treatment of criminality and mental illness, the assessment of abilities and aptitudes, the education of children, the organization of the workplace, and so on.

This merely indicates how psychology positioned itself historically as a natural science but, as such, its continuing concern is the pursuit of objectivity and truth. The psychological theories underpinning therapeutic practices are often broadly understood as scientific in this sense. This strengthens the emphasis on technical expertise, particularly in clinical settings with a biomedical ethos. Ethical considerations are focused on issues relating to applications and professional conduct, following traditional approaches to medical ethics.

However, as Hacking argues, even psychiatric classifications with a possible biological basis, such as schizophrenia, are 'interactive', always open to revision because 'people classified in a certain way change in response to being classified'. Moreover, the very range of competing psychological theories and therapeutic approaches suggests that theoretical concepts, relating to such things as the nature of persons, their well-being, potential and pathology, are value-laden.

Adopting a natural science model of psychology, with its technical expertise model of practice, encourages avoidance of ethical and political debate about the values embedded in such differing therapeutic approaches. It militates against viewing therapy as a fundamentally ethical activity. The natural science model of psychology has, however, been contested from the start. As psychology, history, sociology, economics and social anthropology emerged as empirical disciplines, claims were made that their subject matter is crucially different from that of the natural sciences and requires differing methods of study.

In Britain, John Stuart Mill coined the term 'moral sciences' to distinguish these disciplines. They were termed Geisteswissenschaften in German, which can translate as 'human sciences'. The German philosopher William Dilthey linked the notion of human science to a theory of understanding and he significantly influenced the development of research into human consciousness, subjective experience, meaning and culture.

Consciousness and human agency are emphasized in the human science model, and values are inseparable from its assumption that human beings have the capacity for choice and personal responsibility, as opposed to being entirely determined by internal and external causes. Methods appropriate to the study of self-conscious, reflective and self-determining beings are sought. Nonetheless, in Britain and America, the natural science model predominated throughout the social sciences and psychology, at least until the 1960s.

By that time, in a general climate of humanism generated by political and intellectual upheaval, human science approaches were gaining ground. Humanistic psychology, associated with Carl Rogers and Abraham Maslow and rooted in the European phenomenological tradition, was among them. Its emphasis on free-will and human potential was significant in the political context and counselling first evolved as one of a range of democratizing practices in humanistic psychology. The quality of the therapeutic relationship was stressed together with the validity of the subjective experience and capacity for self-determination and personal responsibility of the person in the client role.

Humanistic psychology, with its stress on values and relationships, remains an important influence. However, while championing human subjectivity and freewill, it courts utopian ideas of democracy and human perfectibility. Rogers, for example, was challenged, from a more existential viewpoint, by May for neglecting the human capacity for evil, and Spinelli contends that humanistic psychology adopts an overoptimistic view of human nature and human freedom. Additionally, the emphasis on 'self-actualization' can lead to a neglect of the self-in-relation, and questions of responsibility to others.

The more general humanism of the early 1960s similarly overemphasized the responsibility of individuals for their own circumstances and life-chances. 'Structuralist' critiques drew upon structuralist linguistics, which defines languages as structured symbolic systems. From this perspective, subjective consciousness, structured by language, could be viewed as socially constructed and more obviously available for scientific study. Human action was understood as generated within symbolic meaning systems in which socio-political power is legitimated in ideologies.

Marxist and feminist studies were particularly important in showing how these power relations are reproduced through the construction of personal identities. As the structures of language and ideology operate, as it were, beneath consciousness, social science renewed its interest in psychoanalytic studies, particularly through the work of Jacques Lacan, who, influenced by structuralist linguistics, claimed, 'the unconscious is structured like a language'. 'Structuralism', again overdeterministic, in turn became a focus of critique, and 'post-structuralism' linked with a broader set of complex and debatable ideas - 'postmodernism' - emerged. It maintains a similar view of the relation between language and consciousness to structuralism, but rejects the conception of languages as large, unified systems in favour of smaller systems or 'discourses' located in specific forms of social life.

Like Weber, post-structuralists and postmodernists argue that life is inherently multifarious and contradictory and all thinking and evaluation limited within perspectives. They contend that grand theories and overarching systems of thought, 'meta-narratives', are oppressive and, in recognizing the varied forms of social life, its 'little narratives', postmodernism has a liberating potential.

Postmodernism and post-structuralism have influenced a range of approaches to the study of human beings that have gained significance in psychology. These approaches include social constructionism, discourse analysis, conversation analysis, deconstruction and critical psychology. Alongside developments in phenomenological research and psychoanalysis, these approaches have contributed much to the study of subjective experience, social relationships and personal identity by rigorous qualitative methods.

Language thus provides a crucial key, unlocking possibilities for studying conscious and unconscious meanings and motivations, culture and ideology. Moreover, the relationship between structure and agency can be explored as a function of how subjective consciousness, while structured by discourses, has the capacity for self-reflection and choice. All this has strengthened the human science model and re-established the significance of critique and the centrality of ethical and political values.

If knowledge is always limited within perspectives, then those perspectives must be made transparent and their implicit values examined. Studies within psychology, which are beginning the self-reflective critique of the discipline, demonstrate that, far from being value-free, psychology plays a key role in constructing and maintaining socio-political structures and power relationships. Michel Foucault's work has been particularly useful in showing how. Psychological theories, viewed as discourses, can be seen to operate within a 'general politics' or 'regime of truth': that is, 'the types of discourse which accepts and makes function as true'.

Consistent with the process of rationalization, in societies like ours 'truth' 'is centred on the form of scientific discourse and the institutions which produce it'. More specifically, studies of the discourses of psychopathology and psychotherapy pose a considerable ethical and political challenge to established therapeutic practice. They show how, whatever the model, biomedical/psychiatric, cognitive-behavioural, psychoanalytic or humanistic, theories situate clients and their problems within normative discourses that, for example, set standards of mental health, adjustment, development or self-realization.

Moreover, they position the therapist as expert and privilege the language of the model over the everyday language of clients. In doing so they often oppress the people they intend to help. An increasing awareness of the limited applicability of technical rational knowledge in therapy, despite the pressure to claim technical expertise, brings into focus value conflicts and the unavoidable responsibility we have to others. Many practice situations are vague and uncertain but decisions must be made and actions taken and accounted for. Social life is, in a real sense, radically open, and socio-political and moral concepts are 'essentially contestable'.

6

Understanding Mental Fitness

Mental health issues can cause young people and their families to be socially isolated. Open access and universal services such as help lines, drug and alcohol services, and leisure services are seen to have a helpful preventative role.

Child-Centered Services

Parents and carers thought services aimed at improving and promoting mental health and psychological well-being needed to be designed specifically with young people in mind. Their comments can be grouped into seven main headings: basic needs, attitudes, services targeted at young people, choice, buildings, advocacy and involvement in planning. All children and young people have a range of basic needs to support mental health and psychological wellbeing. Ideally, these are provided primarily through the family, but for some young people alternative routes are needed to meet these basic needs.

The most important were a sense of belonging, having someone who cares what happens to them, a sense that the world is essentially predictable and benign and feeling that they are understood and have a voice. In addition, parents and carers identified that young people need coping skills, preparation for adult life, help to promote confidence and self-esteem, help in getting their thoughts and feelings across and to know that, whatever the difficulties, their loyalty to their parents will be respected.

From the perspective of parents and carers, the attitude of a service or individual providing a service essentially determines success, far more than skill, qualifications or financial input. The key attitudes were the willingness to listen to young people with open minds, commitment to the young person, honesty, positive attitudes, making people feel wanted and showing understanding and patience.

Many parents and carers felt that some young people are blamed, stigmatised, judged and subject to ignorance, rudeness and blatant discrimination, particularly from health professionals working in generic children's health services. Parents and carers identified key features that, in their opinion, would make it easier for a young person to access a service. The most basic requirement was that services are planned to meet the needs of young people and that any response is based on individual need not service availability. The features felt most important were drop-in services that were informal and confidential.

There is also a need for consistency, both from the individual and from services as a whole. The people providing the service need time to work with the young person and listen to them. This is difficult to provide if the young person feels on a conveyor belt of appointments in a clinic. It is also very important that the adult is reliable and can be trusted by the young person.

Buildings

The physical location and external appearance of services is important. Key features were having buildings that are local, physically accessible and on public transport links. Without easy access, the young person becomes dependent on an adult to take them to the service. It is important that the building is non-stigmatising outside so young people don't feel passers-by or friends will judge them if they are seen going in. The building itself needs to be child-friendly and provide a safe and comfortable environment.

Choice

Parents and carers felt that choice was important for the child or young person. This included a choice of staff and a choice of therapies or medication. It was strongly felt in one group that alternative therapies should be made available within the NHS and that it was unacceptable for parents to be told that the child or young person would benefit from a certain approach but it was only available privately. As part of choice and giving the young person some control over treatment, it was suggested that practitioners need good lateral thinking skills and the ability to look at a whole person.

Treatment plans should be based on good assessment and developed in discussion with the young person and his/her parents or carers. It was noted that fostered children lack some basic freedoms of choice because the foster carer has no parental responsibility and the mechanisms to obtain permission can be unwieldy. Parents and carers had mixed views on their role as an advocate.

Very few parents but more foster carers saw a need for formal and informal advocacy. Both parents and carers talked about a young person's need for peer support and for services to recognise and welcome the involvement and support of a friend.

Involvement in planning

The main reason given for young people needing to be involved in planning was that it is impossible to design appropriate services for children and young people without their input. This was particularly important for children and young people in special circumstances whose needs might be unknown to service planners.

Comprehensive and Equitable Services

Non-discriminatory

Services are not always physically accessible for disabled patients or disabled parents. The generic health professionals refusing to see a special needs patient or being afraid of the young person. Parents asked for recognition that a child with a mental health problem needs the same level of service as a child with a disability. This was particularly relevant to access to respite care services.

On the whole, health services were seen as better co-ordinated than social services. Problem areas included poor communication, poor information sharing, lack of shared values and priorities and territorial attitudes. Sometimes parents even found themselves having to tell staff about other services in the area. While it was important to parents and carers that the child's right to confidentiality was maintained, there was frustration that this was sometimes used to withhold information that was needed to be able to care for the child properly.

The most commonly requested services were:

— respite

— counselling

— access to medication

— twenty four hour, seven day a week support

— psychology

— behavioural support

— play therapy

— self-help/support groups

Parents and carers said there was a general lack of mental health assessments. They wanted rapid access to appropriate services to assess needs and to plan to meet these needs. There were frustrations when a parent or carer's perception of risk differed significantly from the perception of the person carrying out the assessment. Care leavers were seen as particularly vulnerable. Even though services have improved since the Children (Leaving Care) Act came into force, there was still a lack of co-ordinated planning for young people with significant care and health needs.

Parents and carers were concerned about making services and organisations a safe environment for children, with good safer caring practices. Foster carers said that safer care in foster care was related to the ability to make well matched and appropriately supported foster placements. There were concerns that sometimes rigid safer caring policies made it difficult to provide what a child needed in terms of physical contact.

Understanding Mental Illness

As with all types of human experience, no one person's problems, or ways of coping with them, are exactly the same as anyone else's. Some people will have only one of these experiences, others more than one. Some people experience them on only one occasion, others from time to time (for example during periods of stress), and others frequently. Many people who have psychotic experiences also have other psychological, medical or social problems. It is not uncommon for people to have problems with alcohol or drug use, depression or anxiety as well as psychotic experiences. These can arise for the same complex reasons as for any other individual. The combination of psychotic experiences and such difficulties can, however, present further problems.

Many people who have these kinds of experiences do not come into contact with clinical psychologists or psychiatrists because they do not find their experiences distressing. For example, many people hear voices talking to them when there is no-one there, but the voices say relatively pleasant or neutral things so this is not a problem. Some people, however, are so distressed by their experiences that they seek professional help. Some come to the attention of professionals because other people consider their behaviour odd or abnormal.

Traditionally, psychotic experiences have been thought of as symptoms of 'mental illness' such as schizophrenia or manic depression, and the people who experience them have been referred to as 'patients' or ' sufferers'. More recently it has been suggested that there are other ways of thinking about these experiences, and that, therefore, medical terms are not always the only or best ones to use. Traditional psychiatric classifications of psychoses and serious mental illnesses are not necessarily consistent with psychological classifications and descriptions. In order to describe the issues involved , it may be useful to clarify the diffe rent roles of psychiatrists and clinical psychologists.

Psychiatrists are medically trained doctors who specialise in mental health. Clinical psychologists have an academic training in psychology, a n d use this understanding of thought processes, emotion and behaviour to understand and help people with personal difficulties. Despite some differences, psychiatrists and clinical psychologists work closely together. Neverthless, because of their training and background, psychiatrists tend to understand mental health issues in terms of symptoms leading to diagnosis and treatment.

Similarly, because of their training and background, clinical psychologists tend to see mental health issues and psychotic experiences as problems whose causes and solutions will be slightly diffe rent for each individual. Clinical psychologists have, therefore, questioned traditional classifications of psychological distress based on psychiatric diagnosis, and have begun to suggest alternatives. The most frequent diagnoses given to people who experience psychotic problems are schizophrenia and bipolar disorder. Other diagnoses that people might have encountered are;paranoia, psychosis, psychotic illness, delusional disorder, schizoaffective disorder, manic depression and psychotic depression.

Different researchers have recorded different estimates of the incidence of schizophrenia using traditional medical definitions of the problem. Generally there is a consensus that about one person in a hundred will be diagnosed with schizophrenia during their lifetime. The prevalence of the disorder is estimated at between 0. 2 and 1 per cent. It tends first to be diagnosed in early adulthood. This means that, in the UK, between 100, 000 and 500, 000 people are experiencing such problems at any one time.

Schizophrenia is usually reported as slightly more common, and possibly more severe, in men, although this may be in doubt. The majority of men who develop the problems that lead to a diagnosis of schizophrenia do so before the age of 25. Women tend to develop problems about five years later, although there is a ver y high level of variability. Psychiatrists use a number of other diagnoses that are extremely similar to either schizophrenia or bipolar disorder. In general these refer to very similar problems.

Psychotic features are however relatively uncommon, probably represent only some 10 to 20 per cent of inpatients with a diagnosis of depression, and most people, even if they attract such a label, are never admitted to hospital.

Diagnostic Criteria for Schizophrenia

Over the years, the diagnostic criteria for schizophrenia have frequently been revised in order to improve reliability. Following these revisions, very similar rates of the use of the diagnosis of schizophrenia have been revealed in America and the UK. Many different cultures have, it is claimed, terms roughly translatable as 'madness' that describe the common psychotic experiences. However, the social environment generally is a vital part of the picture of many problems, including problems with both physical and mental health.

People living in deprived inner-city areas are much more likely to be given a diagnosis of schizophrenia than people living in more affluent suburban areas. Faris and Dunham's social isolation theorysuggested that poverty and social isolation were likely to trigger psychosis in vulnerable individuals. A second theory, the social drift theor y, suggests that people who are given a diagnosis of schizophrenia might be born in any socio-economic environment. However, the development of psychotic experiences is likely to prove disadvantageous for social functioning and employment opportunities.

People with such problems therefore are likely to drift into lower socio-economic circumstances and end up in poor housing and employment. What is clear is that poverty and the diagnosis of schizophrenia are related, but whether as cause or effect is unknown. There have been a number of studies of the influence of social class on the frequency of the diagnosis of bipolar disorder. Unlike schizophrenia, these have not generally found that a diagnosis of bipolar disorder is associated with social disadvantages.

A number of sur veys have revealed that a sizeable proportion of the general population (including people who have never been thought of as meeting the diagnostic criteria for a mental illness) experience hallucinations. Perhaps as many as one in ten of the general public hear voices regularly. If there are any factors that distinguish 'normal hallucinators' from people who come into contact with mental health services, these would appear to be the distress caused by the experience and the degree to which these experiences are seen as normal

Psychotic experiences not attracting the attention of mental health services. Many people who have psychotic experiences feel that the experiences are very significant in their lives. Some people feel that the experiences have religious or spiritual significance. Some people explain their experiences in terms of supernatural or religious forces, or see the experiences as giving them a deeper understanding of or insight into the world. Psychotic experiences and spiritual experiences.

A diagnosis of a psychotic illness has often been viewed as a cause for pessimism. It is sometimes wrongly thought that psychotic experiences are permanent conditions, with either a recurring or deteriorating course and little hope for the long term. We have heard of instances when patients and their families have been told that there is no chance of recovery and that patients must resign themselves to a life of illness and disability.

The distinction between 'schizophrenia' and 'bipolar disorder' (manic depression) remains a matter of heated debate amongst clinical psychologists and psychiatrists. Outcomes for both diagnoses are enormously variable. On average, people with a classic 'bipolar' picture (that is, episodes of depression and mania with no hallucinations or delusions) have better outcomes than those with a classic 'schizophrenia' picture.

For people who experience a mixture of both types of problem, there is an intermediate probability of a good outcome. In people with diagnoses of both schizophrenia and bipolar disorder, it is clear that outcome is influenced by social factors.

Psychiatric Terminology

In traditional psychiatric terms, the mental illnes 'symptoms' are thought of as manifestations of underlying mental illnesses. The most common diagnostic categories used to classify psychotic experiences are schizophrenia, schizo-affective disorder and bipolar disorder or manic-depression. Many people think that diagnoses serve some very useful purposes, including simplifying communication and permitting a relatively brief and straightforward means of describing complex difficulties. Diagnoses are also used by medically trained doctors as a means of deciding upon appropriate treatment. Some people find having a diagnosis reassuring, because it implies that they are not alone in having the experiences, and gives hope that professionals will be able to help.

The symptom-diagnosis approach to thinking about psychotic behaviour and experiences is well established. Psychiatric diagnoses are labels which describe certain types of behaviour, they do not tell us anything about nature or causes of the experiences. If care is not taken it may be assumed that diagnostic categories offer an explanation for unusual experiences, rather than merely a short-hand description.

The diagnostic approach has not been as useful as was hoped and has been the subject of much scrutiny and debate. In order to understand why, it is helpful to look at the validity of the assumptions underlying the idea and practice of diagnosis. The use of diagnostic categories involves two basic assumptions about consistency and usefulness. If a diagnosis is valid, it should predict prognosis. However, as explained above, the outcome for people with a diagnosis of schizophrenia is extremely variableand attempts to define a diagnostic group with a more uniform outcome have not been very successful.

Diagnoses should also indicate what treatments will be effective. However, responses to medication for 'schizophrenia' and 'bipolar disorder' are also variable. For example, drugs such as Largactil (known as 'neuroleptics' or 'antipsychotics') are often thought of as specific treatments for schizophrenia. But not all people with this diagnosis appear to benefit significantly while some people with a diagnosis of affective disorder (traditionally thought of as unrelated to 'schizophrenia') do benefit.

The effectiveness of lithium, a drug traditionally used with people diagnosed as suffering from bipolar disorder, is similarly variable and non-specific. In one study, people were randomly assigned to either a neuroleptic , lithium, both or neither. It was found that drug response was related to specific problems but not diagnoses:delusions and hallucinations responded to the neuroleptic and mood swings responded to the lithium, irrespective of diagnosis. Diagnostic categories are therefore of very limited use in predicting course or outcome.

Another way of examining the validity of diagnostic categories involves using statistical techniques to investigate whether people's psychotic experiences actually do cluster together in the way predicted by the diagnostic approach. The results of this research have not generally supported the validity of distinct diagnostic categories. For examplethe correlation amongst psychotic symptoms has been found to be no greater than if the symptoms are put together randomly.

Similarly, cluster analysis - a statistical technique for assigning people to groups according to particular characteristics -has shown that the majority of psychiatric patients would not be assigned to any recognisable diagnostic group. Statistical techniques have also highlighted the extensive overlap between those diagnosed with schizophrenia and those diagnosed as having major affective disorder. The central issue in diagnosis is one of classification - the idea that particular psychological problems cluster together and can therefore be considered together.

This has been termed 'carving nature at the joints'. This means that it is assumed that the problems called 'schizophrenia' are different from the problems called 'bipolar disorder' in the same way that birds are different from reptiles. On the basis of the evidence reviewed above, many psychologists believe that these distinctions are invalid, that diagnostic approaches to psychological problems do not reflect real 'joints' in nature.

Psychosis has often been assumed that the behaviour and experiences of people who are placed in diagnostic categories such as 'schizophrenia' and 'bipolar disorder' are qualitatively different from 'normal' behaviour and experience.

A number of clinical psychologistshave suggested that psychotic symptoms lie on a continuum with normality, and are the severe expression of traits that are present in the general population. Individuals range from the conventionally 'normal', through various shades of eccentricity, to those who experience severely distressing psychotic experiences. Thus, the distinction between signs of mental illness (i. e . symptoms) and the expression of human individuality (i. e. traits) becomes blurred. The presence of psychotic-like traits in the normal population has been termed 'psychosis-proneness' or 'schizotypy'.

This continuum view is easily understood if one imagines other common experiences such as anxiety. Individuals differ on how anxious they are in general. This is an enduring characteristic of their personality, and is likely to be due to a combination of genetic factors and their upbringing. Only a minority of individuals will ever experience extremes of anxiety such as a series of panic attacks, which are recognised in the diagnostic textbooks as justifying a diagnosis of an anxiety 'disorder'. Similarly, the state of extreme suspiciousness known as 'paranoia' is on a continuum with the feelings of suspiciousness that we all feel from time to time.

Substantial evidence has accrued in favour of the idea that psychotic experiences are on a continuum with normality. So-called 'schizotypal' traits have been described which are believed to have similarities with thought processes observed in psychotic experiences. These can be measured in 'normal' individuals by the use of questionnaires. Such questionnaire studies have demonstrated that there is a wide range of scores in the normal population, and that schizotypal traits tend to form clusters similar to different sorts of psychotic experiences.

Moreover, individuals who score highly on such scales resemble individuals with psychotic experiences on a number of psychological measures, such as measures of attention and reasoning. Recent psychiatric research has indicated that a dimensional approach to psychotic experiences can be more useful in terms of understanding and planning care than a categorical system.

Symptom approach

Many researchers have argued that the problems of diagnosis can be overcome by focusing on specific experiences and behaviours (symptoms, in medical terminology). In Britain, in particular, considerable progress has recently been achieved in understanding specific psychological mechanisms that can lead to unusual beliefs, hallucinations and difficulties in communication.

Psychological formulations

In order to understand and explain people's experiences, clinical psychologists have developed the approach termed 'formulation'. Psychological formulations are a way of helping people to make sense of their difficulties in a way that is meaningful to them. They comprise a statement of what the person sees as the problem (or problems), how these might have come about, and what is keeping them going.

Problems will usually be expressed in terms of what the person experiences (such as unhappiness, hearing voices, not functioning well at work, or fearing that people are trying to harm them) rather than in terms of 'symptoms' observed by others. Clinical psychologists also attempt to develop, in collaboration with the client, ideas about what things might have led to the development of these problems.

Typically, a formulation will examine what events happened in a person's life, and how they have and reacted to these. This can help the person some of their problems have not just come 'out blue' but may be an understandable response to circumstances. Even when it is not possible to one particular cause, worker and client can explore together what might be maintaining the problem. Formulations tend the psychologists and their clients learn more problems. Formulations are designed to be 'best about the problems, and these guesses are tested time.

Psychologist and client work together develop a picture of the problems and a joint theory what has caused them, and what might help. Psychological case formulations are complex. Clinical psychologists draw on a large variety of psychological theories, each drawing on scientific research. individual case formulation will not draw on all research, each person may have a range of interrelated psychological difficulties.

Traditionally, psychiatry has taken a more biological tack, reflecting the medical basis of the profession. This pattern is changing, however. Some psychiatrists are rapidly becoming more focused on social issues. Many are becoming champions of Cognitive Behaviour Therapy (a form of psychological therapy) and are therefore increasingly examining psychological causes of their patients' distress. Similarly, clinical psychology has a tradition of seeing distress (including psychotic experiences) as stemming principally from aspects of an individual's psychological make-up.

Increasingly clinical psychologists are developing a stance that sees things more in terms of interactions as described above. Thus clinical psychologists recognise influences of biology on the way in which people interpret events in their lives, as well as emphasising how apparently reflex or 'natural' processes can be influenced by expectation or experience. They are also becoming increasingly aware of the impact of the social environment on the development of psychotic experiences.

Clearly the nature and causes of psychotic experiences will remain complex and mulitifactorial even when we know more. Over time, we will learn more about the different causes, and how they interact. A single cause of 'schizophrenia' will not suddenly be identified. Moreover, even in the highly unlikely event that the cause of any one person's psychotic experience was ever to be known with scientific clarity, this truth would not hold for everyone. Clinical psychologists therefore respect the individual's own experience and perspective.

In order to try to make some sense out of this complexity, clinical psychologists attempt to focus on the way in which people make sense of their experiences. Psychologists tend to assume that people who report psychotic experiences are either having unusual perceptual experiences (that is they are experiencing things like hallucinations that are, in themselves, unusual) or are interpreting normal experiences in an unusual way (perhaps having strange intrusive thoughts that appear alien). Of course, it is entirely possible that both events are occurring.

Clinical psychologists then attempt to account for why people might have unusual experiences and why they might interpret things in an unusual way. Unusual experiences sometimes occur for medical or biochemical reasons - people can become delirious when ill and can hallucinate when they have taken street drugs. For some people it is possible that physical problems with the structure or functioning of the brain might lead to abnormal experiences. Physical influences like street drugs can also create unusual experiences.

For other people, psychotic experiences might arise from misinterpretations of normal events. For instance, it is possible that paranoia might develop if you tend to read malevolent intent into other people's behaviour. It is also possible that you might begin to believe that aliens are talking to you if you misinterpret your internal speech as not being your own. Psychologists are interested in why these sorts of interpretations of events might develop. Experience and research in a wide range of psychological problems such as depression and anxiety have clearly demonstrated that traumatic, abusive or unpleasant events during a person's childhood can affect the way that the person interprets information later in life.

An example might be people who grow up in a school environment where they are persistently bullied. Those people might develop beliefs that they were worthless, that other people are likely to harm them, and that the world is a callous and unfeeling place. There is evidence that many people who have psychotic experiences have experienced abuse or trauma at some point in their lives.

It is widely assumed that psychotic experiences have some kind of biological cause , although precisely what this is may not yet be clear. Such views have become more prominent over the last two decades, and tend to be reported uncritically by the media. The stress-vulnerability model suggests that both psychological and biological factors may leave some people more vulnerable than others to environmental stressors.

Genetic factors are likely to be important, but should not be thought of as providing a complete causal explanation for psychotic experiences. Evidence for a genetic element to psychotic experiences comes mainly from studies that compare identical and non-identical twins and from adoption studies that compare the biological and adoptive relatives of people who were subsequently given a diagnosis of schizophrenia or bipolar disorder.

The closer the biological relationship, the greater the risk of a relative also having the diagnosis. The best estimate is that the risk of being given a diagnosis of schizophrenia is 46 per cent for the child of two parents with the diagnosis, 13 per cent for the child of one parent with the diagnosis, and 9 per cent for siblings. This is compared to the overall risk of 1 per cent for the general population. It is clear that psychotic experiences tend to 'run in families'. However this is not necessarily due to genetic causes.

There are numerous problems in trying to disentangle genetic inheritance from environmental factors such as upbringing. In the studies relating to 'schizophrenia', doubts have been raised about methods of determining the genetic similarity of the twins, the length of time adopted children had spent with their families of origin, and the mental health status of some of the adoptive families.

A major recent study from Finland compared the adopted children of mothers with a diagnosis of schizophrenia with a group of adopted children whose biological mothers did not have the diagnosis. The first group was found to be more likely to contain people with more severe diagnoses, including that of schizophrenia. However, clear differences between the two groups were only found where the adoptive families were rated as 'disturbed'. All children, even those who were believed to be carrying some genetic vulnerability, did well in 'healthy' adoptive families.

In other words, families seemed to play a crucial role both in increasing, and protecting against, genetic risk. It was noted that this genetic risk may well consist of a 'nonspecific' predisposition, a kind of general sensitivity to the environment, which leads to the development of serious psychopathology only under unfavourable psychological circumstances. '.

Biochemical abnormalities

It has been argued that if genetic factors do have a role in causing people to have psychotic experiences, they do so through biochemical abnormalities. The dopamine hypothesis - the theory that schizophrenia may result from overproduction of the neurotransmitter (brain chemical) dopamine - has been extensively researched over the last 20 years. This theory is based on two observations. First, some neuroleptic ('anti-psychotic') drugs affect the chemical dopamine and can induce Parkinsonism (abnormal movements similar to those seen in Parkinson's Disease).

Parkinsonism is known to be related to low dopamine levels. Second, drugs such as amphetamines, which increase dopamine production, can also produce psychotic-like experiences. However, neither of these statements allows us to draw definite conclusions about cause. The first argument (about the effect of dopamine-influencing medication) is rather like arguing that headaches are caused by lack of aspirin. Nor does the theory explain why symptoms improve only gradually on neuroleptic medication, although the drugs have an immediate effect on dopamine in the brain.

Secondly, the possibility that taking amphetamines CAN lead to psychotic experiences does not mean that chemicals (whether taken as drugs or already existing in the brain) are their only or main cause. The new 'atypical' neuroleptics such as clozapine affect a different neurotransmitter - serotonin - rather than dopamine. Researchers are now investigating the possible role of serotonin in psychotic experiences. Similar arguments have been made about the role of neurotransmitters (especially serotonin and noradrenalin) in producing the extreme changes in mood and activity that lead to a diagnosis of bipolar disorder.

The fact that people with a diagnosis of schizophrenia are more likely to have been born in the early months of the year has been put forward as evidence for some environmental influence at work. Difficulties during birth and exposure to viruses in the womb have also been suggested as factors, but so far such hypotheses remain speculative.

More recent technological approaches have examined patterns of blood flow and patterns of electrical activity in the brain. The results suggest that different types of psychotic experiences are associated with different patterns of activity. In particular, low levels of activity in the frontal lobes of the brain have been observed in people experiencing 'negative symptoms'. However, the differences between people with and without a history of psychotic experiences are usually modest, with a large o verlap between the groups.

In most studies the people with a history of psychotic experiences have also taken powerful medication for many years, and this is not always taken into account. It is also possible that life experiences, psychological trauma, severe distress, and psychotic experiences may themselves leave physical traces on the brain, as well as the other way round. For instance, recent research has indicated that practice at complex memory tasks actually makes parts of the brain grow in size.

There are, of course, biological and brain events that correlate with all aspects of our mental functioning. This is equally true for 'normal' and 'abnormal' experiences. However, it is incorrect therefore to conclude that biological abnormalities are the primary causes of a complex range of experiences. The undoubted existence of biological aspects to our experiences does not in itself justify categorising them as medical illnesses.

Few people would wish to deny that there may be some kind of inherited tendency to break down under stressful conditions. It is the nature of this tendency that is under dispute. It is likely that it may be a widely-distributed and non-specific trait such as temperamental sensitivity.

As in most areas of human life, research into the causes of psychotic experiences indicates that both biological and environmental factors are important. As might be expected, these two broad types of factors interact. Moreover, no one single cause has been identified, and it is likely that many aspects of an individual's life are significant in producing psychotic experiences. This idea has been described as the 'stress-vulnerability' model. In the stress-vulnerability model, it is suggested that everybody has a different level of vulnerability to the development of psychotic experiences.

People are believed to be more or less vulnerable as a result of both biological factors (which could well be the result of either genetic factors or biological changes following birth) and psychological factors (for instance, being very sensitive -or resilient - to stress in a psychological rather than biological sense). Sensitivity to particular stresses may, of course, be at least partly a result of events that have happened previously in the person's life.

In the stress-vulnerability model, it is suggested that vulnerability will result in the development of problems only when environmental stresses are present. If the vulnerability is great, relatively low levels of environmental stress might be enough to cause problems. If the vulnerability is lower - the individual is more resilient -problems will develop only when higher levels of environmental stress are experienced.

The World Health Organisation has reported that psychotic experiences occur in many different cultures, and appear at least superficially to be similar even when the cultures are very different. People in different cultures describe psychological problems in different ways. For instance, in some cultures, some psychological problems might be described in terms of physical pain or discomfort, in other cultures such experiences are described using emotional terms such as fears or anxiety.

Cultural patterns may also influence the ways individuals explain their experiences. Unpleasant or upsetting experiences are often explained using the common cultural beliefs. Sometimes explanations used by people from ethnic minorities can be misinterpreted as psychosis if the context is not understood. In some cultures, for example, many people believe in the possibility of being possessed by demons. Sometimes someone's belief that he or she is possessed might be wrongly thought to be a psychotic or 'delusional' belief.

People of African Caribbean origin living in the UK are three times more likely to receive a diagnosis of schizophrenia than are white people. It has been suggested that the racism and social exclusion which black people living in Britain often experience may increase the likelihood of developing psychotic experiences. These sociocultural aspects of vulnerability to psychosis are likely to have much in common with other experiences of abuse and marginalisation and require further investigation. Black people are also more likely to receive a diagnosis of schizophrenia than white people even if the experiences they describe are the same.

We all deal with many stressful events in our lives;birth, death, divorce, moving house, taking an exam. Such life events are generally thought to be stressful even if they are positive; even winning the lottery could produce stressful life changes. At their worst, life events can either be traumatic, or shade into ongoing 'hassles', or chronic stresses.

The idea that families cause psychotic experiences, or more specifically that parents are responsible if their children have psychotic experiences, was popular in the 1960s. A term 'schizophrenogenic mother' was even developed. Not all carers are relatives; some individuals live in hostels, for example, and have important relationships with staff and other carers.

Cognitive Deficits

Cognitive 'deficits' are general impairments in processes such as perception, memory and attention. The word cognition is simply another term for 'thought'. They are often thought to be caused by brain damage or physical abnormalities, although they might also be the result of people's experiences such as trauma or an impoverished environment. Temporary 'deficits' can also result from depression, demoralisation, or poor motivation.

Cognitive 'biases', on the other hand, are said to be present when people notice, pay attention to or remember some types of information better than others. For example, it has been known for some time that depressed people tend to notice and recall negative information more than people who are not depressed. Similarly, different people interpret information differently. This can lead to biases.

Again, people who are depressed tend to interpret information in a negative way. For example, they see the glass as half-empty, not half-full. Because cognitive biases cannot usually be accounted for by general deficits (because some types of information are processed normally) they are unlikely to be the consequence of brain damage.

Traumatic, abusive or unpleasant events during a person's childhood can affect the way that the person interprets information and reacts to events later in life. People who have psychotic experiences very commonly report having had highly distressing or traumatic life experiences such as bereavements, abuse and assault. The common themes appear to be extreme threat, abuse or events that lead to overwhelming emotions. Understandably, such events will affect the way the person sees the world.

Everybody interprets new events and challenges in the light of previous experience. Abusive, threatening or overwhelming events are likely to lead to feelings of powerlessness and expectations of more abuse. One metaphor that has been used is that of a lock and key. If the key fits the lock, the door can be opened. If your psychological perspective includes feelings of powerlessness and expectations of abuse, a street mugging might have particularly dramatic consequences.

All events, including psychotic experiences, will be interpreted from the perspective that the person has developed. People therefore respond differently to life challenges, and also in the ways they understand and make sense of psychotic experiences.

Until recently, most cognitive research into psychotic experiences has focused on people with a broad diagnosis of schizophrenia. This work has focused almost exclusively on cognitive deficits. There is good evidence that some people with a diagnosis of schizophrenia have difficulties on a variety of measures of attention. For example, there is evidence of difficulties for some people in the very earliest stages of processing visual information.

Many people with a diagnosis of schizophrenia appear more easily distracted than people who do not have psychotic experiences. A number of researchershave suggested that difficulties in understanding other people's behaviour might explain a number of psychotic experiences. It is generally believed that ordinary social behaviour depends on our ability to use other people's actions and conversation as clues for understanding what they might be thinking.

Some people who are having psychotic experiences appear to show difficulties with this skill, although it seems to improve when the experiences become less distressing. It is possible that these difficulties are related to the very high levels of stress and confusion that sometimes accompany psychotic experiences.

One early theory of 'schizophrenia' was that it reflected a 'loosening of connections' in the brain. (That idea actually led to the use of the term 'schizophrenia' meaning 'fragmented mind'). Psychotic experiences such as hearing voices, unusual beliefs and 'thought disorder' appear to involve making unusual connections between apparently unrelated events. This is not in itself either good or bad. Sometimes making unusual connections between things is valuable, when it is termed 'lateral thinking' or 'creativity'.

In fact, people who score highly on measures of 'schizotypy' also score highly on measures of creativity . It is even possible to imagine how the ability to make Cognitive deficits seem to be associated with psychotic experiences and vulnerability to psychotic experiences, rather than with 'schizophrenia'. Whenever comparisons have been made between people with a diagnosis of bipolar disorder and people with a diagnosis of schizophrenia on these kinds of cognitive tests, few differences have been found.

Most research on cognitive deficits has involved broad diagnostic categories such as 'schizophrenia' and 'bipolar disorder'. Because of the problems with these diagnoses, and because such deficits do not fully explain psychotic experiences, many clinical psychologists have begun to investigate the psychological processes which may be involved in particular experiences. Considerable progress has been achieved in this respect over the last ten years, and only a few of the most important findings can be mentioned here.

Many studies have shown that people who have unusual or delusional beliefs tend to 'jump to conclusions' when faced with limited or contradictory information. By comparison, people who do not hold such beliefs tend to be more cautious when evaluating evidence. The two most common kinds of unusual belief that people report are the fear that people are trying to harm or kill them and the belief that they have special powers or abilities or that they are famous or powerful.

Studies suggest that these unusual beliefs are associated with specific biases in reasoning about social situations. The evidence suggests that many people who experience paranoia have a general tendency to assume that other people cause the things that go wrong in their lives. Some researchers have argued that these kinds of beliefs therefore have a defensive function although this claim remains controversial.

Cognitive biases and hearing voices

Most people often experience an 'inner voice' when thinking in words (for example, when deciding what to do, or when struggling with a problem). There is evidence that some people who experience verbal hallucinations (voices) have difficulty distinguishing their inner speech from speech from an external source. Some of this evidence has emerged from physiological studies (for example, brain scanning experiments) in which it has been shown that speech areas in the brain are active when people hear voices. Some psychological experiments show that some people who hear voices experience difficulty when they are asked to distinguish between their thoughts and words spoken to them.

Incoherent speech ('thought disorder')

Although incoherent speech has traditionally been

regarded as a symptom of 'schizophrenia', studies show that it occurs more frequently in people experiencing maniaand reflects a difficulty in adjusting speech to the needs of the hearer. Most people only become thought disordered when emotionally stressed and, for most of the time, their speech is perfectly coherent.

Mania

Mania is a term used to describe a complex cluster of 'symptoms', which includes grandiose delusions, increased activity, incoherent speech and, in most cases, a paradoxical combination of both positive emotions (euphoria) and negative emotions (depression and irritability). People experiencing mania sometimes believe that they are particularly famous or important. These beliefs are traditionally termed grandiose delusions.

Recent studies have suggested that they are associated with patterns of thought similar to those seen in paranoia. Both paranoia and mania might play a role in protecting self-esteem. Some researchers think that the increased energy and activity seen in people experiencing mania may sometimes be caused by disruption of the physiological mechanisms that control the sleep-wake cycle.

Occupational and Social problems

People with psychotic experiences sometimes have problems in their social lives. They may have problems in continuing with their work, which may have serious effects on their general well being. These social problems can be analysed in more detail for the purposes of designing support and therapy. For instance, if it is known that the person has difficulty communicating, they might decide to improve their skills or alternatively they may wish to take part in activities, occupational and leisure, which do not require high levels of these skills.

Insight

'Insight' is a controversial area. Insight traditionally refers to the agreement of the patient that they have a diagnosable mental illness. Since many people (including many clinical psychologists) feel that 'diagnosable mental illnesses' are highly dubious concepts, it seems odd to insist that people share one view of their problems. However, insight can also be interpreted, more reasonably, as the willingness or ability of the person to accept that they have acted differently during an episode of psychotic experiences compared to their 'normal' behaviour. This may allow the person to engage with services to prevent such problems in the future that may interrupt or interfere with their lives.

A range of drug treatments is commonly prescribed for people who have psychotic experiences. The most important are 'antipsychotic' drugs. These drugs were first developed in the late 1940s and have since been regarded as the preferred medical treatment for psychotic experiences. There are many of these drugs including chlorpromazine, thioridazine, trifluoperazine, sulpiride, haloperidol, flupenthixol, and fluphenazine. Recently, a new class of 'atypical' neuroleptics (for example clozapine, risperidone and olanzapine) has come into use.

Neuroleptic drugs may be used in the acute phase of psychosis. Afterwards, they can be used either intermittently (when the person feels unwell, distressed or under stress) or prophylactically (when the person has partly or totally recovered in order to try to prevent further episodes). For many people, prophylactic treatment can be important in preventing further episodes and hospital admissions. However, some people wish to avoid long-term drug treatment and prefer to use nonmedical approaches for coping with psychotic experiences or to use medication only at times when the experiences are distressing.

There is little evidence that any neuroleptic is superior to others. Claims have been made for the superior efficacy of clozapinebut these have been made on the basis of trials of short duration, and/or with comparison doses of conventional neuroleptics that have been less than optimal. A typical neuroleptics seem at least as effective as the traditional medications. A preference for atypical neuroleptics over 'typicals' may be justified because of their less severe EPSEs. Atypical neuroleptics do, of course, have their own range of potential adverse effects. These can include weight gain and lethargy.

Poor compliance with neuroleptics has been cited as an important cause of continuing illness and further hospitalisation. Noncompliance is often attributed to lack of insight (the individual does not understand or refuses to accept that she/he has an 'illness'). However:

(a) People's beliefs about their experiences are complex, and cannot be reduced to a simple dimension of insight. For example, some prefer to think of their problems in psychological terms rather than embracing the medical model.

(b) The strategies that people take in order to manage their medication are also complex. Many people are neither compliant nor noncompliant but vary their medication according to circumstances.

(c) For many people, the balance between the advantages of n e u roleptic treatment (for example, a reduction in the f requency or intensity of psychotic experiences) and the disadvantages (for example, a d verse effects) is a fine one.

(d) People who refuse neuroleptic drugs completely do so for a variety of reasons. In one study it was found that some refused because they perceived their drug treatment to be ineffective and some because they were distressed by adverse effects. Only a few gave reasons that were judged to be psychotic.

(e) In general levels of 'noncompliance' with psychiatric medication are similar to those in the physical health field and the reasons for noncompliance are also similar. For these reasons it is wrong to assume that it is always rational to comply with neuroleptic treatment. Any constructive approach towards ensuring that people receive optimum medical treatment must take into account people's views on and personal experience of their drug treatment.

Drug treatment should always be based on a collaborative relationship between prescribers and patients. Mental health service users should be able to make appropriate choices about their own medication. Prescription has traditionally been seen as a process in which doctors make the decisions and patients follow. Professionals take a more collaborative stance, which enables service users to play a more active role. Specific approaches that may be useful include:

(a) Giving people information about the benefits and hazards of treatment.

(b) The use of simple behavioural strategies such as diaries and reminders to help people remember when to take their drugs.

(c) 'Compliance therapy' is based on the approach known as 'motivational interviewing' which is often used in substance misuse services. A recent study of this approach found that it led to improved adherence with medication and a better outcome in terms of global functioning. However, others have argued that such approaches do not sufficiently take into account the fact that not everyone benefits from medication. Each individual needs to be able to make an accurate appraisal for him or herself of the benefits and costs of taking medication.

(d) Other drugs may be prescribed in addition to or instead of antipsychotic drugs. In some parts of the world, it is common to offer people short courses of benzodiazapine medication (e. g. valium) in order to reduce anxiety in the short term prior to determining whether treatment with a neuroleptic is necessary. Antidepressant medication may also be prescribed if appropriate.

(e) If, having considered all the relevant information, the service-user decides not to use medication, this decision should be respected and he or she should continue to be offered support by mental health services. We view with considerable concern the practice adopted by some clinicians of equating such a decision with 'refusing treatment' and withdrawing support as a result.

Mood stabilisers

Mood stabilising medication may be prescribed for people who experience excessive mood swings, especially mania. The most common mood stabiliser is lithium carbonate. More recently, it has been discovered that anticonvulsant medication, for example carbamazepine, can have mood stabilising effects, although these have not been as thoroughly evaluated.

Common adverse effects of lithium treatment include nausea and diarrhoea in the short term. These symptoms often subside after a few weeks. Longer term effects include tremor (often affecting the fingers), increased production of urine (sometimes disturbing sleep and leading to thirst), weight gain and hypothyroidism (suppression of thyroid function). Adverse effects of carbamazepine can include drowsiness, dizziness, nausea and double vision.

The effectiveness of mood stabilising medication has been less well evaluated than the effectiveness of the neuroleptics. Although it is widely believed that prophylactic medication can prevent future episodes of illness, especially in people who have experienced mania, most of the clinical trials that have been conducted with lithium have suffered from quite serious methodological limitations.

A recent study found that about 50 percent of people treated with lithium experienced severe mood swings during a one year period. Discontinuation of lithium is often followed by a manic episode. However, it is not clear that this is caused by the re-emergence of 'illness'. It is possible that this phenomenon is a kind of 'rebound' effect. Consistent with this theory, it has been found that a manic episode is more likely following rapid discontinuation of lithium compared with a tapered reduction of medication.

Long-term adherence with lithium therapy is often poor, but this is often because of the unpleasant side effects. As in the case of neuroleptic medication, adherence is most likely to be achieved if there is a collaborative relationship between patient and prescriber, and if the person is adequately informed of the benefits and costs of medication. Cognitive behavioural methods similar to those used in the management of neuroleptic medication have a role in helping people to achieve the best from lithium therapy.

Psychological interventions are usually used in conjunction with medication. Some people, however, prefer to use alternatives to drug treatments for psychotic experiences. Other people may find medication helpful when in acute distress, but do not want to take it long-term. Some psychologists feel that psychological interventions could offer an alternative to long-term medical treatment for some people.

The integration of medical, psychological and practical approaches echoes the growing recognition that social and psychological factors interact strongly with biological factors in psychotic experiences. Many individuals with psychotic experiences have complex difficulties. The psychotic experiences themselves, the framework within which people understand them, their coping responses as well as the disruptions of relationships and social networks, and the depression and anxiety that can follow are all important.

All these demand a careful therapeutic response. In addition, special emphasis has recently been given to implementing 'early intervention' services for people showing the first signs of psychotic experiences. Finally carers often experience substantial burdens, and sometimes also need help.

Currently, most people who have psychotic experiences and receive talking treatments also receive medication. However, research in the United States has suggested that for some people, psychotherapy can be more effective without medication, and that it can sometimes be more effective than medication alone. There are several different psychological, psychosocial and psychotherapeutic approaches. These all have slightly different names and slightly different emphases. There are important differences between approaches. Different approaches may be more or less suitable for different people, and some psychologists or therapists prefer to work in one way rather than another. However, there are more similarities than differences between these different 'brand-name' approaches.

In the past there has sometimes been a degree of antipathy between different 'schools' of therapy. However, this is changing. Part of the reason is the increasing recognition on all sides of the importance of the subjective meaning of psychotic experiences. The value, common to all therapies, of the opportunity for people to talk and think about their experiences in a calm, supportive and non-judgmental atmosphere is also increasingly being recognised.

Sometimes the onset of psychotic experiences can be traumatic and lead to major life changes:emotional support and the opportunity to talk is very important. All psychological interventions should be based on a trusting, collaborative working relationship between the professional and the client. It is possible that this is often the main 'active ingredient'. It is certainly vital, and it is important that service users should be able to find a therapist or worker with whom they feel comfortable.

Social Skills Training (SST)

Social skills training (SST) aims to address the interpersonal problems that are sometimes associated with psychotic experiences. It appears to be relatively successful, with benefits maintained for long periods. However, its benefits do not appear to generalise, and the benefits may not always last. Some people who have psychotic experiences also experience problems with concentration, attention, memory and thought processes. These can affect relationshipsand treatment outcome.

Cognitive remediation attempts to help people improve their performance through practice and rehearsal. The evidence for its effectiveness is mixed. There is a well-known relationship between engagement in meaningful occupation and health status, both in the general populationand in those with mental health problems. Occupational therapyand specific programmes for vocational rehabilitationmay be beneficial. There is evidence that employment may have a greater positive impact than any other single factor.

Some people experience distress or confusion to that the extent that they need ongoing support in order to live the kinds of lives they want to lead. For example, some people may need reminding about things. Others may need practical help such as provision of meals, or emotional support if they experience severe anxiety or frequent low mood.

Personality Disorders

Some people who have been given a diagnosis of a 'personality disorder' are more likely to commit serious violent offences, especially if they use alcohol or street drugs. Personality disorder is a category under the current Mental Health Act that is the basis for the detention of 'mentally disordered offenders'. More specific diagnostic labels commonly used include 'antisocial personality disorder' and 'psychopathic disorder'. Neither of these terms are related to psychotic experiences, but to people who are believed to be abnormally aggressive or anti-social.

This definition is circular. That is, people may receive the diagnosis because their behaviour is considered aggressive or anti-social and then their violent and antisocial behaviour is seen as being a product of the 'disorder'. In this light, it is not surprising that the diagnosis of 'psychopathic disorder' predicts dangerousness. There has been considerable government concern at this, resulting in draft proposals for the care and treatment of people given such diagnoses.

A recent large scale study in the USAhas demonstrated that people recently discharged from psychiatric care pose no general greater threat of violence than any of their neighbours. However, those who abuse drugs or alcohol are more of a risk than people with a drug or alcohol problem who have not received a psychiatric diagnosis. Variables other than psychotic experiences are much better predictors of violence.

These include: alcohol and drug abuse;being male;being young;social exclusion; and past history of violence. If you wanted to predict whether a person was going to be violent in the future, the most important factor to consider would be whether they had been violent in the past. Whether or not they had a diagnosis of mental illness would be less important than their alcohol or drug use, their age, their gender and their social circumstances and their relationship to the potential victim.

Risk of suicide

Although it receives less publicity than homicide, suicide is a much more common for people with a diagnosis of mental illness. Successive governments in recent years have set suicide reduction targets as a measure of improving mental health. The problem of increased risk of suicide for people with psychiatric problems remains a real concern for users themselves and for those working in mental health services.

As with violence, factors other than diagnosis are predictors of suicide (e. g. unemployed status, previous selfharm, chronic physical health problems, and the availability of the means of self-harm).

Risk of self-neglect

In addition to the risk of suicide, the confusion or disorganisation that can sometimes accompany psychotic experiences can put people at risk. For example, some people are at times unable to organise themselves sufficiently to maintain an adequate diet. Someone who is confused is also likely to be at risk of exploitation and abuse from other people .

The risk of service contact

All treatments bring with them the risk of adverse effects. The negative effects of psychiatric drugs are well documented. These problems are often under-recognised and understated by professionals and the general public. Some people also at times become distressed when receiving psychological therapies.

Mental health services have been associated in the past thirty years with mistreatment, triggering a series of official inquiries into their functioning. The mistreatment has included emotional and physical neglect and abuse. Women on mixed-sex psychiatric wards are very frequently at risk of sexual assault and exploitation. In the USA there have been a number of law suits against therapists relating to the sexual or emotional exploitation of clients.

Even when properly conducted, psychological therapies often involve talking about painful issues that can be distressing. It is important that people are adequately informed about what is involved before making a commitment to beginning therapy.

Bibliography

Anderson, H. & Goolishian, H., "The client is the expert: A not-knowing approach to therapy. In S. McNamee & K. J. Gergan (Eds.). Therapy as social construction. London: Sage Publications, 1992

Baillie, A. & Corrie, S. "The construction of clients' experience of psychotherapy through narrative, practical action and the multiple streams of consciousness", Human Relations, 49 (5), 295-311, 1990.

De Vauss, D. A., "Surveys in social research (4th ed.)", Australia: Allen & Unwin, 1995.

Dinnage, R., "One to one, Experiences of psychotherapy", London, Penguin, 1988.

Drier, O., "Client interests and possibilities in psychotherapy", In Critical psychology-contributions to an historical science. Cambridge, England: Cambridge University Press

Drier, O. "Re-searching psychotherapeutic practice", In S. Chaiklin & J. Lave (Eds.). Understanding practice. Cambridge, England: Cambridge University Press, 1993.

Giorgi, A., "An application of the phenomenological method in psychology", In A. Giorgi, C. T. Fischer & E. Murray (Eds.). Duquesne studies in phenomenological psychology, (pp. 82-103). Pittsburgh, USA: Duquesne University Press, 1975.

Giorgi, A., "Phenomenology and experimental psychology: 1. The Review of Existential Psychology & Psychiatry", 5 (3), 6-16, 1985.

Kuehl, B. P., Newfield, N. A., & Joanning, H., "A client-based description of family therapy", *Journal of Family Psychology*, 3 (3), 310-321, 1990.

Lewis, K. N., Epperson, D. L., & Foley, J., "Informed entry into counselling: Client's perceptions and preferences resulting from different types and amounts of pretherapy information", *Journal of Counseling Psychology*, 36 (3), 279-285, 1989.

O'Connor, T., Meakes, E., Pickering, M. R., & Schumann, M., "On the right track: Client experience of narrative therapy", *Contemporary Family Therapy*, 19 (4), 479-495, 1997.

Pinsof, W. M., "A conceptual framework and methodological criteria for family therapy process research", *Journal of Consulting & Clinical Psychology*, 57 (1), 53-59, 1989.

Pinsof, W. M. & Wynne, L. C., "The effectiveness and efficacy of marital and family therapy: Introduction to the special issue", *Journal of Marital & Family Therapy*, 21 (4), 341-343, 1995.

Rennie, D. L., "Toward a representation of the client's experience of the psychotherapy hour", In G. Lietaer, J. Rombauts & R. Van Balen (Eds.). Client-centred and experiential psychotherapy in the nineties, (pp. 155-172). Belgium: Leuven University press, 1990.

Sells, S. P., Smith, T. E., & Moon, E., "An ethnographic study of client and therapist perceptions of therapy effectiveness in a university-based training clinic", *Journal of Marital & Family Therapy*, 22 (3), 321-339, 1996.

Spinelli, E., "Demystifying therapy", Great Britain: St Edmundsbery Press, 1994.

Index